UNITED STATES ARMY

This We'll Defend

UNITED STATES MARINES

Semper Fidelis

UNITED STATES NAVY

Non Sibi Sed Patriae

UNITED STATES AIR FORCE

Aim High
Fly, Fight, Win

UNITED STATES COAS

Semper Paratus

In Loving Memory

of

_____

PRESENTED BY

_____

_____

_____

Date

From a Grateful Nation

Our lives are bound at every turn to other people. We live in groups and usually do what we can to make the life of the group a little better. No where is this more evident than in the United States Armed Forces. Whether your loved one served one tour of duty, or provided decades of service, there is a unique and unbreakable bond among those who served. It is one of the few professions that require a commitment to a cause greater than one's own life. The profession of arms revolves not around the tangible rewards associated with other endeavors but rather around the intangible virtues of duty, honor and service.

Military service often comes with extreme hardship, suffering, separation from family and trauma not only to service members but also to their loved ones. It may also bring a sense of fulfillment and pride rarely achieved in other vocations. Your loved one was part of this distinct group of men and women who, at one time, stepped forward and said, "I will serve."

Many, if not most veterans, go on to meaningful and rewarding careers after their service. Veterans contribute to society in an untold number of ways and their time in uniform helped define them. Traits and skills learned are easily transferable and much needed in society. More importantly than job skills, however, are the traits veterans learned while serving: courage, commitment, selflessness, tenacity, the list continues. Veterans have been tested, many on the battlefield, on or under the sea and in the skies above.

In this volume we honor the many Americans who have served, and in doing so made great sacrifices; some even the ultimate sacrifice, so that we all might live free.

★ONE WHO SERVED

A MEMORIAL TRIBUTE TO YOUR VETERAN

A Memorial Tribute & Keepsake Volume

ACKNOWLEDGEMENTS

TEXT

John Sydney Tighe
Robert P. Giers
BMCM (SW) Edward F. Gallagher, IV. USNR, Retired

PRODUCTION

John Addy

GRAPHIC DESIGN & ILLUSTRATION

Abby Pelicano, Christopher Pelicano

DEDICATION

This book is dedicated to all those who have protected our freedom by their service in the United States Armed Forces; and to their families, whose constant love and support have helped strengthen and sustain them in that duty.

Photographs on pages 58-59 and 61 are Courtesy of U.S. Army.

GOOD WILL PUBLISHERS, INC.
Gastonia, North Carolina

ISBN: 978-0-9833218-0-4

Contents

Paying Tribute ...

★

A Tribute and Keepsake

The Purpose and Use of this Book

This volume is designed as a tribute, a keepsake and an aid for the family. It is a document of your love and remembrance for someone very dear to you as well as a tribute to all who have served our country with honor. The volume is a keepsake in which you are invited to record pieces of family history through a family tree and through selected journal entries relating to your life with your loved one and others. In a way, this book is a celebration of commitment, love and sacrifice. And finally, because grief is a natural process, this volume may come to your aid as you live through the deep sorrow that accompanies the death of a loved one. It may even serve as a companion along the way.

To have been a veteran of the United States Armed Forces is to have been a contributing citizen in a unique way. It is to have been part of a great delegation of humanity willing to give of themselves, sometimes in far away places and sometimes in harm's way, but always as a living symbol of the importance of individual sacrifice for the common good. It is to have loved one's country. It is this love and sacrifice that we honor and it is in your loss that we send you our deepest sympathy. In the mournful notes of *Taps* we not only bid a veteran farewell, but we also pay tribute to a well-lived life and a well-deserved rest.

Honoring our loved ones who have passed away is a natural component of human behavior and can therefore help us through difficult times. It is the sincere desire of the publisher that in some small way we may, in the gift of this book, touch your heart in a time when so many of us feel so alone. We hope this keepsake tribute will not only aid you in your loss but also aid you in celebrating life, especially the life of your dear one who served.

Paying Tribute . . .

To Pay Tribute ...

Remembering One Who Served

The Great Longing. Throughout recorded history we humans have grieved the passing of one of our own. The religions of the world have all variously defined the great longing in the human heart to reach beyond this mortal life. Because of the inevitability of death, the act of remembering deceased loved ones has always been a way to hold the life of another in our minds. Those associated with the military might perhaps have a better notion of this tradition than others. The families of veterans understand in a unique way that memory is a great teacher. What we share as humans is the innate need, the great longing to remember those we have loved.

The particular qualities that endeared a loved one to us can and should be passed on to others, stories of the bends and curves and blind corners of a life; stories of triumph and service, of duty and honor. Our loved ones live on in the hearts and minds of those who are left. The great longing is really for an undying connection to those we love. Their character does not perish, but lives on in those who have been affected by it.

In the following section we offer a record of the life of your loved one. It is a place to set down the dates, the times, the images and the thoughts that make up your loved one's legacy and that will keep an eternal flame in your heart and in the hearts of future generations.

The Blue Star Banner

An Important Symbol

The blue star service flag is a familiar banner displayed by the families of those serving their country in the armed forces. The gold star banner is an indication that the family has lost a loved one in the service of their country. Many families today also incorporate a silver star for those wounded or injured in war zone duty.

In World War I, U.S. Army Captain Robert Queisser designed the banner in honor of his two sons, who were then in service. As Captain Queisser was in the 5th Ohio Infantry, the people of Ohio responded to the design by using it themselves. In a short time it became an official banner, to be used by the families of all American service members to the end of World War I and on into World War II as well.

The banners have become popular once again with our troops deployed in active duty so many places around the globe. Traditionally, the banners were displayed in the windows of the family awaiting the return of their service member. Its symbolism has struck a deep chord with families today as a patriotic response to the needs of one's country, standing for service, for courage and for loyalty. It is a silent and simple but profound and powerful emblem of a familial connection to all those who serve their nation as well as a solemn reminder of all the brave souls who have served in the past so that we may live as free citizens.

★

A Tribute

In this section you are invited to remember your loved one in some very special ways. A record of the funeral service itself is provided for those who, in years to come, will see how, when and where you bade your loved one farewell. A place for a photograph of your loved one will, of course, become one of the family treasures you pass on. You will find a place to list some very special friends who attended the funeral. Your recollections in *The Times of Your Life* journal pages may someday provide for family members an inspirational keepsake unlike any other. We have also included a Family Tree as a way to pass on to younger members of the family a sense of continuity that may help strengthen familial bonds as they grow older. Adding a record of your loved one's civic and military service as well as a service photograph to this very personal documentation is a befitting tribute to one you have loved and will remember always. To pay tribute to your loved one in thought, memory and a record of family life is a way of passing on the love and affection that will always be in your heart.

The Funeral Service

for

_____

Name of Deceased

SERVICE

_____

Location

_____

Officiating

_____

Date

BURIAL

_____

Cemetery Name

_____

Date of Internment   *Section*   *Lot*

INURNMENT

_____

Date and Location

Tribute Portrait

*Place Keepsake
Photograph Here*

Special Friends in Attendance

_____   _____

_____   _____

_____   _____

_____   _____

_____   _____

_____   _____

_____   _____

_____   _____

_____   _____

_____   _____

_____   _____

★

The Stream of Time

*"Time is but the stream
I go a fishing in."*

Henry David Thoreau

In his brief quote, Thoreau described well the process of remembering. Memory can be a great gift when vivid recollections comfort our aching hearts. To cast a line of memory into the stream of time and pull up hallowed moments can be a healing act. The remarkable endeavors, the prominent desires, the cherished dreams, fulfilled or not, are all the ingredients of an individual's life worth unveiling for those left behind.

In the following journal lines you may travel back to your first meeting with a loved one. You may recall a special person in a crisp uniform of one of the armed services, the hopeful laughter of another time and place, or any number of special moments together. In the record of a first meeting between couples who will spend their lives together, or between a parent and newborn child, or among closest friends, there truly is something special. Those recollections may be well worth retrieving from the recesses of your mind. We have provided here pages for more of that journey back: a survey of a year or a snapshot of a moment, a description of a memorable event or a few written words as witness to a blessed and honorable history. It is yours for the writing, your stream in which to drop a line.

The Times of Your Life

Journal Pages

_____

_____

_____

_____

_____

_____

_____

_____

_____

_____

_____

The Times of Your Life

Journal Pages

★
Our Family Tree

It has been a long standing tradition in families to keep track of ancestors and descendents by making a record of them in a family keepsake. Most families have one or more people who delve into the genealogical records and try to keep tabs on family history. These folks usually collect family stories as well as photographs and memorabilia, which are, of course, invaluable. Personal family keepsakes make genealogists of us all, for a treasured keepsake is a record of the heart, tracking the virtues and the character that make families special.

For the one who served, there may have been specific stories or keepsake items that always recalled that service in a unique way. Those stories and keepsakes, as well as the service itself, continue to be meaningful beyond all words. In this section you are invited to trace your roots in a way that may someday be handed down to an interested family member. Family histories always remind us of the continuity of life and therefore how blessed we are with family. We hope that you are able to find strength in your family tree, for it can serve as a chronicle of those blessings and help you live through the sorrow that is always a part of true love.

Family Register

MARRIAGE

_____

Date   Location

HUSBAND

_____

Name

_____

Date of Birth   Birthplace

_____

Died   Date / Location

WIFE

_____

Name

_____

Date of Birth   Birthplace

_____

Died   Date / Location

★

Children & Grandchildren

_____
Name   Spouse

_____
Child's Name   Child's Name

_____
Child's Name   Child's Name

_____
Child's Name   Child's Name

_____
Name   Spouse

_____
Child's Name   Child's Name

_____
Child's Name   Child's Name

_____
Child's Name   Child's Name

_____
Name   Spouse

_____
Child's Name   Child's Name

_____
Child's Name   Child's Name

_____
Child's Name   Child's Name

Children & Grandchildren

_____
Name   *Spouse*

_____
Child's Name   *Child's Name*

_____
Child's Name   *Child's Name*

_____
Child's Name   *Child's Name*

_____
Name   *Spouse*

_____
Child's Name   *Child's Name*

_____
Child's Name   *Child's Name*

_____
Child's Name   *Child's Name*

_____
Name   *Spouse*

_____
Child's Name   *Child's Name*

_____
Child's Name   *Child's Name*

_____
Child's Name   *Child's Name*

Military & Civic Record

Military Branch   _Military Specialty_

Dates of Service   _Rank_

Service Highlights

Post-Service Memberships/Activities

Armed Services Photograph

Place Keepsake
Photograph Here

★

Beyond Military Service

Every veteran has a life beyond their military service. Whether the veteran completed one tour of military duty or retired after decades of service, the vast majority of them went on to productive lives outside the military. While the majority of this volume concentrates on military service and the veteran's family, this section is designed to record information for future generations about your loved one's life after the service. What did your veteran do for a living after the service and what companies provided this employment? What titles and promotions were achieved and did this employment involve different locations or even different states? What were your veteran's civic involvements, hobbies and special interests? Beyond mere facts, this section is designed to "complete the picture" of a person for his or her descendents. While filling out this information, ask yourself two questions, "What personal information do I wish I knew about my ancestors and what information would my deceased loved one want descendants to know?"

_____

_____

_____

_____

_____

THE UNITED STATES ARMY

THE UNITED STATES MARINE CORPS

THE UNITED STATES NAVY

THE UNITED STATES AIR FORCE

THE UNITED STATES COAST GUARD

To Remember ...

Honoring All Who Served

A Grateful Salute. To honor those who served our country is to say thank you for their sacrifices. It is to pay homage to their willingness to stand for an idea and their courage to give themselves for that idea. The idea is freedom and a long line of brave souls have, with brains and brawn, merit and might, long suffering and loyalty, fought to keep that idea the central characteristic of our democracy. To honor those who served is to respect what they served for. It is less about rank and decoration as it is about dignity; less about glory and more about the esteem due those who saw duty as the lifeblood of our nation. Let us honor them still. Let us stop one in uniform and say "Thank you for your service." Let us with our families stop on occasion to pray for the safe return of those who serve us now in the far corners of the world. Let us honor all who serve now and all who served before them.

In the following section we salute the armed forces in general and the great national symbols that reflect the willingness of veterans to give even the ultimate sacrifice for their country. We salute all who served.

★

The Price of Freedom

The price of freedom is always high but also necessary if America is to preserve the unique rights of her citizens. The cost of our freedom is measured not only in dollars and resources but also in the blood sacrificed by the brave members of our military forces. It is not only the casualties tallied and the outward wounds and resulting scars that comprise that price; many veterans endured situations so terrifying that they returned from war different people, forever changed. Yet the dictates of global conflict and the particular needs of the military services continue to determine when and how the sons and daughters of America serve. Every veteran who served honorably or who is serving now deserves our special thanks for their essential role in the preservation of American freedoms.

The right of free speech, the freedom to worship as we please, the right to assemble, the right to a speedy trial, protections against self incrimination and unreasonable search and seizure, these are just a few of the freedoms granted us by our Constitution in the Bill of Rights.

In many foreign lands, these freedoms do not exist. Yet, since the time of the Revolutionary War, our armed forces have sacrificed to ensure that our rights are protected and that Americans remain free. Many of those who served can recall the moment they joined the service and repeated the U.S. Armed Forces Oath of Enlistment which begins with the following words:

"I, (NAME) do solemnly swear (or affirm) that I will support and defend the Constitution of the United States against all enemies, foreign and domestic; that I will bear true faith and allegiance to the same..."

For over two hundred years, our armed forces have defended our way of life. From the Revolutionary War to our most recent conflicts, men and women of the armed forces have answered their country's call and have given their all, many making the ultimate sacrifice of their very lives. But those who came home carried in their hearts a love for America and a commitment to her, a commitment we are here proud to honor.

★

What is a Veteran?

The term "veteran" refers to an individual who has served in any of the armed forces of the United States. In the United States individuals enlist or are commissioned into service. Service is divided into two periods of time, "Active Duty" and "Reserve". "Active Duty" is full time service whereas "Reserve" status can be either active (certain weekends and several weeks of active duty a year) or inactive, which is essentially a standby mode without active participation. Mobilized Reservists have been utilized extensively since the attacks of September 11, 2001.

Officers and enlisted personnel both undergo initial training. Every individual is required to undergo testing for physical, mental and moral suitability for the armed forces. Once completed, the individual will be assigned to advanced specialty training in a specific field which will generally be the assigned classification in military service.

At the end of the active duty term, the individual has a choice of leaving active duty or becoming re-affiliated with their chosen branch. Should the individual choose not to remain, the term of their obligation will expire and they will be discharged from the service. It should be noted that while this individual is a veteran, they are not "retired" from the service. The term "retired" is reserved for those veterans who have normally completed twenty or more years of service.

Each veteran has faithfully served for the good of our country and in the defense of our nation. While others have enjoyed the freedoms of America, the veteran is the one who helped provide those freedoms. While others enjoyed the comfort of their families every night, veterans had to separate from their families to stand watch in foreign lands. While others prospered, the veteran is the one who provided the security for that prosperity without financial gain. Yet often, the veteran has been rewarded in ways that many others will never understand. Pride, Duty, Honor - these are the hallmarks of a veteran's character. Pride in measuring up to the demands of the service, dutifully carrying out assignments given, even when they may place one in harm's way, and the honor of representing the freedom for whom so many have given so much. This is a veteran.

★

The Home Front

The Families that Stay Behind

For every service member that deploys, loved ones keep a vigil at home. For the deployed member, thoughts of family and friends are constant.

While the family is not subjected to mortal risk, the emotional strain is nonetheless daunting. The absence of a loved one for an extended period is difficult, especially when children are involved. The spouse must be mother and father. There are bills to pay, activities to attend, and the ongoing attempt to keep life as normal as possible. If a loved one is deployed to a war zone, families carry a constant burden of fear and uncertainty. Because information is readily available on the web and family members are able to search for news of missions, units, offensives, accidents and casualties, the information age can be a blessing and a curse.

The armed forces do an excellent job with casualty assistance. In the event of the death of or injury to a service member, a casualty officer will visit the family before news is released. Every knock on the door, every phone call, every vehicle that comes to a stop in front of the home, brings potential news that families dread, that their loved one has been killed, wounded or is missing in action.

Ours is a voluntary force and military members and families understand all too well the sacrifices that will be required during deployments, and even during training. Military spouses bond together, support groups offer assistance, children talk among themselves about the wonderful day when Mom or Dad returns. Families send packages, letters, pictures and gifts to their loved one. This active involvement in the deployment brings with it comfort in the knowledge that "a little taste of home" is on the way.

The sacrifice made by military families will never be understood by those who have not lived it. But as long as men and women who wear the uniform remain prepared to step forward, those who love them will support them, wait for them, love them, and pray for their safe return. If the military is bonded with the cement of duty, honor, country and service, so too is the military family.

United States Armed Forces
The Order of Precedence

The armed services of the United States are the Army, Marine Corps, Navy, Air Force and Coast Guard. The order of precedence is the sequence in which these services appear. Placement is determined by service birthdays beginning with the Army on June 14, 1775; however, there are two notable exceptions.

The first is the Navy and Marine Corps. The Navy was formed nearly a month before the Marine Corps and both represent the establishment of the Continental armed forces (Continental Navy, etc.). After the Revolutionary War, services were reestablished as the United States armed forces. The Marines always maintained their 1775 inception date but the Navy utilized several later dates as their service anniversary. By the time the Navy officially returned to their earlier date of inception in 1775, the order of precedence had been in place for nearly half a century; as a result, the original order of precedence (with the Marine Corps before the Navy) remains to this day.

The second exception is the Coast Guard and Air Force. The Coast Guard was established in 1790, well before the Air Force, which did not become an independent armed service until after WWII (previously it was the Army Air Corps/Forces). However, the other armed forces are in the Department of Defense, while the Coast Guard is under the Department of Homeland Security (previously under the Department of Transportation). Only when the Coast Guard operates as part of the Navy, such as in time of war, does it move before the Air Force in order of precedence.

The armed forces order of precedence highlights the importance of historical tradition. The following historical overviews follow their various evolutions as our nation united against the crown, battled its way through infancy, and suffered the precious blood of sons and daughters.

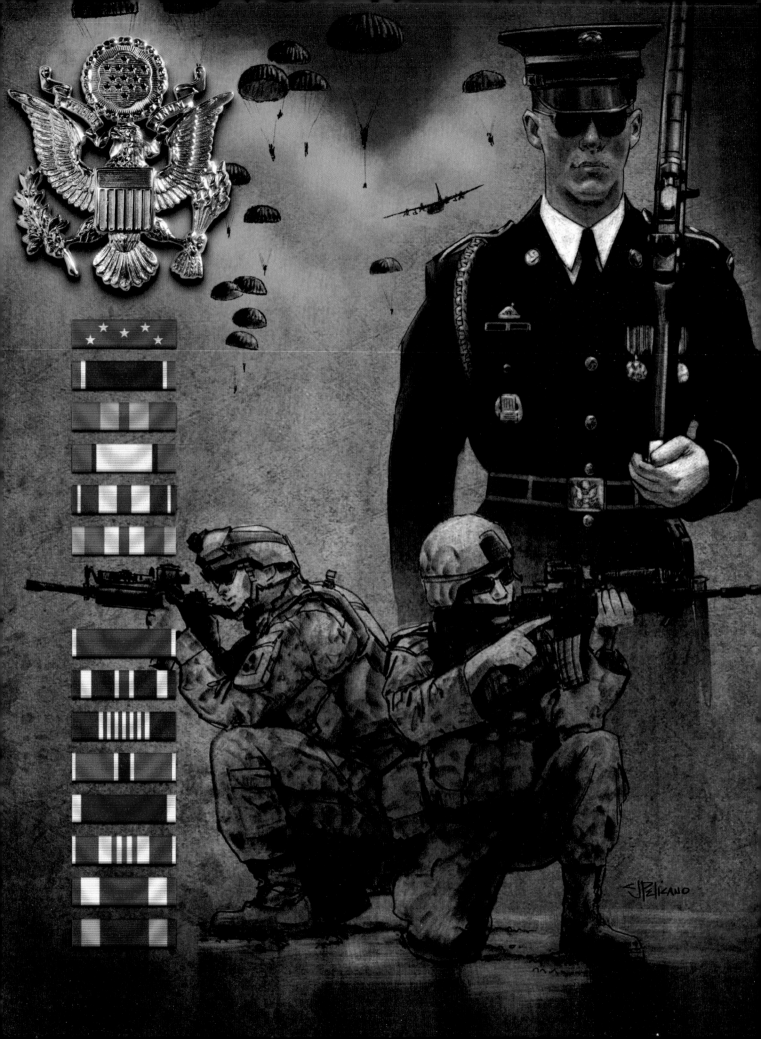

THE UNITED STATES ARMY

From Continental Army to Counterinsurgency

The first of America's armed forces was the Continental Army of 1775. It was made up of former British army soldiers and members of colonial militias. Under the leadership of George Washington, it was quickly embroiled in battle against British forces, employing what would later be called guerilla tactics to hack away at British forces and their mercenary allies. The Continental Army ultimately succeeded and at the Treaty of Paris, the independence of the United States was recognized.

In 1791 a standing army was established. In the war of 1812 the ground army stood strong, and scored a major defeat of British forces. For the next decades the Army skirmished with Native Americans who were trying to halt the rush of settlers migrating west. It also fought the Mexican-American War, which gained for the United States an enormous amount of territory.

With the Confederate States of America opening fire on the Union-held Fort Sumter in Charleston, South Carolina, the bloodiest war in U.S. history began. The superior industrial strength of the north and sheer number of Union troops afoot, brought decisive end-of-war victories in Gettysburg and Vicksburg. After the Civil War, Army victories in the Spanish-American War and Philippine-American War gained much additional land for the U. S.

In World War I, Army troops helped breach German lines, aiding the ultimate victory for the allied forces of Britain, France and Russia. The United States joined World War II after the attack on Pearl Harbor. Army forces eventually helped capture Sicily and North Africa and army soldiers by the thousands engaged the enemy courageously on D-Day and in battles leading to the subsequent defeat of German

★

THE UNITED STATES ARMY

forces and the ultimate liberation of Europe. In the Pacific, the Army and the Marines seized control of the Pacific Islands from Japan.

The Cold War with the Soviet Union saw hundreds of thousands of U.S. Army troops stationed throughout Europe. Hundreds of thousands of Army troops fought to avert an occupation of South Korea by the Communist forces of North Korea but a cease-fire returned Korea to its pre-existing state. By 1965, large numbers of U.S. Army troops were being deployed to Vietnam. In traditional battlefield confrontation American forces were decidedly victorious and in the TET Offensive severely weakened the enemy. But domestic political pressure and opposition forced a U.S. withdrawal in 1973 and the war's end in 1975.

In the 1980's, the U.S. Army was once again an all-volunteer force and began preparing troops for the growing technological revolution. In 1990, Iraq invaded Kuwait and U.S. land forces were subsequently deployed. In 1991, Operation Desert Storm saw troops, many of which were U.S. Army soldiers, driving out Iraqi forces in a remarkably adept and impressive victory that took less than one hundred hours. Direct combat action subsided somewhat after Desert Storm, although Army troops were used in various peacekeeping efforts, including a U.N. mission in Somalia and a NATO peacekeeping force in Bosnia-Herzogovina.

Following the terrorist attack on the U.S. on September 11, 2001, the U.S. and NATO invaded Afghanistan, displacing the government of the Taliban. The U.S. Army also participated in the 2003 allied invasion of Iraq, capturing and bringing to justice Saddam Hussein. This conflict, as well as that in Afghanistan, evolved from a more traditional form to that of a counterinsurgency, including large numbers of suicide attacks and roadside bombs, resulting in thousands of U.S. casualties. Operation Iraqi Freedom and Operation Enduring Freedom together have cost thousands of American lives.

THE UNITED STATES ARMY

U.S. Army troops, including thousands of National Guardsmen and mobilized reservists, have lately endured longer deployments and uniquely rugged conditions of the Middle East, to offer what they have offered from the very first battles of the Continental Army: their courage and their strength, their superior training and combat expertise, their undying love of their country and, in some cases, their very lives.

The Army Commendation Medal

The Commendation Medal of the US Army was first cast in 1945. The decorations are presented to Army service personnel for acts of heroism and meritorious service. For valorous action reflecting direct contact with an enemy force, the Valor Device "V" may be attached to the decoration. The Bronze and Oak Leaf clusters are affixed to denote subsequent awards.

THE UNITED STATES MARINE CORPS

From Revolutionary War to Global Force in Readiness

The 1775 Continental Congress established the Continental Marines, marking the inception of the United States Marine Corps. Though the first Marines distinguished themselves greatly, with the end of the Revolutionary War the force was dismantled to be formally re-established in 1798. The Marines took part in many subsequent operations, such as against the Barbary pirates along the "Shores of Tripoli".

In the War of 1812, Marines fought alongside Andrew Jackson in the defeat of the British at New Orleans. During the Mexican War (1846-1848), Marines joined General Winfield Scott's army fighting all the way to the "Halls of Montezuma." Marines also served in the Civil War, at Bull Run and with the blockading squadrons at New Orleans and in the Carolinas.

Following the Spanish-American War (1898), the Corps entered an era of expansion and professional development. In World War I, the Marine Corps distinguished itself heroically on the battlefields of France and Marine pilots flew bomber missions over France and Belgium. More than 30,000 Marines served in France and more than a third were killed or wounded. By the end of World War II, Marines had become expert practitioners of amphibious warfare and had grown to include six divisions, five air wings, and supporting troops. Their forces reached as high as 485,000 and, at war's end, 82 Marines had also earned the Medal of Honor.

The Korean War again highlighted Marine valor, especially in amphibious assault. Marines endured year after year of offensive and counter-offensive strategies and guerilla warfare initiatives, until the last Marine ground troops were extracted in 1955. Marine involvement in Vietnam began in 1965, and by 1968 Marine personnel reached nearly 85,000. As the South Vietnamese began to assume a larger role in the fighting; marine

★

THE UNITED STATES MARINE CORPS

presence subsided and the last ground forces left Vietnam by the summer of 1971. The Vietnam War was the longest engagement in Marine Corps history and thousands of untold acts of courage and patriotism were never known to the public.

In recent years, Marines have assumed a significant role in NATO's presence throughout northern Europe. The 1980s brought terrorist attacks on U.S. embassies internationally and Marine Security Guards served with distinction in the face of this challenge as well as in Granada and Central America, among other areas. The 1990 Iraqi invasion of Kuwait, saw the Marine Corps deploy its largest force since World War II in Operation Desert Shield. 1991's Operation Desert Storm, again, called on Marines in an overwhelming defeat of Iraqi forces. Soon after 9/11, Marines were operating in southern Afghanistan as part of Operation Enduring Freedom and they continue to play a key role in the Global war on terrorism. Expeditionary Forces entered Iraq in 1991 as part of Operation Iraqi Freedom. Marine units continue to provide air and ground support to operation Enduring Freedom in Afghanistan as well as in Iraq.

Around the world deployments have demonstrated the Corp's ability to respond quickly to humanitarian emergencies. From hurricane relief efforts to search and rescue and disaster recovery operations, such as in Louisiana and Mississippi in the aftermath of hurricanes Katrina and Rita, the Marine Corps is always ready whenever and wherever the nation calls.

From the Revolutionary War to the World Wars, as well as Korea, Vietnam and more recent and current deployments, Marines continue to earn their motto of Semper Fidelis (Always Faithful). In Iwo Jima during World War II, a single image of the Marine Corps became fixed in the minds of Americans. The defining moment occurred where, despite devastating casualties, Marines fought inland and continued to the top of Mount Surabachi. There a photograph was made of five Marines and one Navy Corpsman raising a Stars and Stripes to replace the small original flag that had been placed on the mountaintop. That image of the flag raising came to symbolize the spirit, courage and determination expected of every Marine. Always prepared to deploy anywhere in the world, accomplishing whatever type of mission assigned, today's Marine Corps is truly a vigilant "force in readiness." With a firm resolve also to face tomorrow's challenges; it continues its long tradition and proud heritage of faithful service to the nation.

The Marine Corps Commendation Medal

In 1943, the Navy began offering Commendation Medals, presented for acts of heroism and meritorious service and available at the time as ribbons. The actual medal was added to the ribbon in 1960 and the United States Marine Corps shared the decoration with the Navy until 1994 when it was renamed the Navy and Marine Corps Commendation Medal. Valorous action associated with the medal and representing direct contact with an enemy force, allows the wearing of the Valor Device "V" on the decoration. Silver and gold Award Stars denote the attainment of additional awards.

THE UNITED STATES NAVY

From Fledging Service to Naval Superpower

It took the Continental Congress of 1775 to authorize the building of ships that would become the United States Navy. Throughout the Revolutionary War, ships defended ports and impeded the movement of British ships full of soldiers and supplies. They also battled British warships at sea. These operations and John Paul Jones's raids on British coastal communities gave the fledgling service a reputation for valor.

European examples quickly showed the United States the importance of maintaining a navy, if only to protect a neutral's rights at sea. In 1798, Congress established a Navy Department to manage the new fleet. By 1812, the navy's heroic deeds ensured its survival for another generation.

The U.S. Navy grew up during the Civil War, developing new gun and steam propulsion technology that made it the most modern and effective sea-going force in the world. In a time of increasing technological growth, the U.S. began the building of steel battleships. Competent seamen were being trained as well as commissioned officers. Against the Spanish fleet in 1898, the "New Navy" won dramatic victories at Manila and Santiago Bays.

In 1917, the U.S. Navy adapted successfully to the challenges of convoys, troop transport, and antisubmarine warfare systems. Before it was over, the nation had joined with the Royal Navy to escort over 2 million men and supplies that aided the Allies to victory.

Following World War I, a smaller navy learned to adapt new technologies to enhance capabilities. The navy concentrated on improving gunfire, on submarine warfare and on carrier based aviation. In the Depression of the 1930s, President Roosevelt and Congress began building ships to jump

★

THE UNITED STATES NAVY

start the economy as well as to counter the growing military forces in Germany and Japan. Fortunately for the U.S. our aircraft carriers avoided the devastating raid on the fleet at Pearl Harbor and two of the greatest naval battles ever—at Midway and the Philippine Sea—were fought by naval aviation.

After World War II, U.S. naval supremacy would not be challenged. With the advent of the nuclear submarine, naval ships joined bombers and intercontinental ballistic missiles as one leg of a nuclear triad that would help define cold war parameters. The surface navy remained centered on the aircraft carriers. In Vietnam carriers were supplemented by river gunboats for some of the most dangerous operations of the war.

The Soviet Union's fall left the U.S. Navy without a rival. Nonetheless, carriers and amphibious capabilities were refocused for the expeditions and police actions the United States continues to face, as the only global superpower and the finest sea power in existence.

Naval Special Warfare also developed from the World War II era underwater demolition teams into today's Navy SEALS, Special Boat Units and Explosive Ordinance Disposal teams. Navy construction battalions, known as Seabees, have evolved into the Navy's premier engineers and builders.

The Navy Commendation Medal

In 1943, the US Navy offered its first Commendation Medals. They are awarded to service personnel for acts of heroism and meritorious service. The Valor Device "V" is worn on the decoration if the act or acts being recognized represent direct contact with an enemy force. US Navy silver and gold Award Stars point to the earning of additional awards.

THE UNITED STATES AIR FORCE

From the Wright Brothers to World-wide Engagement

Three-and-a-half years after the Wright brothers flew the world's first powered airplane, the U.S. Army Signal Corps formed an Aeronautical Division. The Aeronautical Division accepted delivery of its first airplane from the Wright brothers in 1909 and a small band of early Army Airmen formed the 1st Aero Squadron, in 1913.

World War I saw the major combatants with already developed aircraft industries. In response, President Wilson created the Army Air Service and placed it directly under the War Department. By the time of the armistice in November 1918, American industry had produced nearly 12,000 aircraft and American Airmen had distinguished themselves both in Allied units and as part of the American Expeditionary Forces (AEF).

U.S. air power came of age in World War II under the Army Air Forces (AAF). Expansion of the AAF accelerated after Pearl Harbor and it oversaw deployment of the largest air armada of all time and air power helped make possible the Allies' total victory over the Axis powers. The U.S. Air Force won its independence as a full partner with the Army and the Navy in 1947 just as test pilot Chuck Yeager broke the sound barrier, launching the new Air Force into the supersonic era.

Air Force units provided the cornerstone of North Atlantic Treaty Organization (NATO) capabilities for the next four decades and in the 1950s, the Air Force's Strategic Air Command (SAC) became the preeminent instrument of American defense strategy. Soon, with the development of launch vehicles and orbital satellites, the Air Force mission also expanded into space. In Vietnam military aviation performed in a wide variety of roles from aerial combat to close air support. The Air Force also

★

THE UNITED STATES AIR FORCE

became the designated branch for Combat Search and Rescue of downed pilots and other compromised personnel behind enemy lines.

In the 1970s, the Air Force modernized its aircraft and missiles while continuing to expand its role in space. It also made great progress on satellite-based communications, reconnaissance, warning, weather and navigation systems.

In recent years the Air Force's well-trained personnel and sophisticated weapons lived up to a vision of global reach during Operation Desert Storm and Operation Desert Shield where the Air Force helped win one of the most lopsided battlefield victories in military history. Air power allowed coalition ground forces to liberate Kuwait and quickly drive into Iraq with fewer casualties than those suffered by the United States in a typical week of the Vietnam War.

Without the Soviet threat, the post-Cold War Air Force has been called upon for increased participation in contingency operations, such as humanitarian and peacekeeping operations in places like Somalia, Rwanda, Haiti and the Balkans and to help to stop a barbaric civil war in Bosnia.

Today the pace of technological change moves ever faster while America's role in protecting against aggression and fostering world democracy is more complex. Key roles in Iraq and Afghanistan have kept the entire Air Force either in a deployed or support role in the fight against terrorism at home and abroad. Today's Air Force looks eagerly to the future while remembering the lessons and achievements of a storied and heroic past and in building what is now the world's only truly global air and space force.

THE UNITED STATES AIR FORCE

The Air Force Commendation Medal

The US Air Force created its own version of the Commendation Medal, for acts of heroism and meritorious service, in 1958. Two years later it added the medal to the ribbon award. If the valorous action that earns the Air Force Commendation Medal is performed in direct contact with an enemy force, the Valor Device "V" may be worn on the decoration. The Air Force denotes additional awards of these military ribbons with bronze Oak Leaf Clusters.

Coast Guard

THE UNITED STATES COAST GUARD

From Maritime Law to Security at Sea

In seniority, the Coast Guard is the oldest continuous sea-going service of the United States. It was created on 4 August 1790 when Congress passed a bill, written and submitted by Alexander Hamilton, the Secretary of the Treasury, to create a "system of cutters" to enforce the new nation's customs' laws, that at the time were the only source of revenue for the federal government. Now one of the country's five armed services, the United States Coast Guard is a unique agency of the federal government. Known variously through the nineteenth and early twentieth centuries as the Revenue Marine and the Revenue Cutter Service, the Guard expanded in size and responsibilities as the nation grew. Though "cutter" used to point to a certain very defined type of sailing vessel, it now refers to any Coast Guard vessel over sixty-five feet in length.

The Service received its present name in 1915 under an act of Congress when the Revenue Cutter Service merged with the Life-Saving Service. The nation then had a single maritime service dedicated to saving life at sea and enforcing the nation's maritime laws. Aviators were also engaged in this activity and the service's first involvement in aviation was when Life-Saving Service personnel from the Kill Devil Hills Lifesaving Station assisted Orville and Wilbur Wright during the world's first heavier than air flight at Kitty Hawk, North Carolina, on 17 December 1903.

The Coast Guard began to maintain the country's aids to maritime navigation, including operating the nation's lighthouses, when President Franklin Roosevelt ordered the transfer of the Lighthouse Service to the Coast Guard in 1939. In 1946 Congress permanently transferred the Bureau of Marine Inspection and Navigation to the Coast Guard, thereby placing merchant marine licensing and merchant vessel safety under its control.

★

THE UNITED STATES COAST GUARD

The Coast Guard is one of the oldest organizations of the federal government and, until the Navy Department was established in 1798, served as the nation's only armed force afloat. The Coast Guard continued to protect the nation throughout our long history and have served proudly in every one of the nation's conflicts. The Coast Guard may boast of a World War II Medal of Honor winner in the person of Signalman First Class Douglas Munro, who, after volunteering to evacuate a detachment of Marines on Guadalcanal, placed himself and his boats to serve as cover for the last men to leave. He was fatally wounded after gallantly protecting these last men. His final words were, "Did they get off?"

National defense responsibilities remain one of the Coast Guard's most important functions to this day. Even when other services are not actively engaged in battle, Coast Guard personnel are never out of harm's way because of the ongoing need for rescue at sea and the ever dangerous and unpredictable nature of drug interdiction and anti-terrorism duties. The Coast Guard now operates as part of the Department of Homeland Security, serving as the nation's front-line agency for enforcing our laws at sea, protecting the marine environment and our vast coastline and ports, and saving life. In times of war, or at the direction of the President, the Guard serves under the Navy Department.

Whatever particular mission it is given, the United States Coast Guard has served the welfare of the country with intelligence, determination and valor. Its place in the annals of American history will be ever as a stalwart protector of the nation and a saver of lives.

THE UNITED STATES COAST GUARD

The Coast Guard Commendation Medal

In 1943, the US Coast Guard authorized the creation of a Commendation Medals. It was available as a ribbon only until 1960 when the service added the medal to the ribbon. The Commendation Medal is presented for acts of heroism and meritorious service. Should the valorous action have been performed in direct contact with an enemy force, the Valor Device "V" may be worn on the decoration. Coast Guard silver and gold Award Stars denote additional awards.

★

Three National Symbols

The Bugle Call, the Monument and the Resting Place

The somber notes of *Taps*, sounded by a distant bugler are a call to a final resting place, either heard at a loved one's graveside with the American flag draped and then folded for the family, or felt in the deepest recesses of one's heart, they still reverberate with meaning in days of great sorrow.

While some service members on duty conclude another exhausting day, others begin their work, standing watch and patrolling sea, sky and land in the dead of night. *Taps* does indeed signify the end of day and a time to rest. But not for all. And so too, as your loved one is laid to rest, thousands of others remain vigilant, continuing a tradition that dates back to the founding of our union. It is only fitting that the lovely strains of Taps, reflective of both vigilance and the time of rest, are also used as a final salute to one who served.

Twenty-five to thirty times a day, families of those who have served their country hear that emblematic bugle call at a new graveside in Arlington National Cemetery where over 300,000 other markers fill the hallowed landscape. It would be difficult, if not impossible, to find a veteran who did not regard Arlington with a special reverence. For it is here that a virtual sea of white tombstones mark the final resting place of fellow veterans who served their country or even gave their lives for it.

Designated as a military cemetery on June 15, 1864, Arlington contains not only veterans from the civil war to the present but in fact has veterans from all our nation's wars, beginning with the American Revolution. Also, some of our nation's most well known women veterans are interred at Arlington including Dr. Anita McGee, the first female army surgeon who founded the Army Nurse Corps in 1900 and Major Marie Rossi, a helicopter pilot killed one day after the cease fire that ended Operation Desert Storm. They represent just a fraction of the brave women who have served America in uniform.

Now Taps ...

★

Three National Symbols
The Bugle Call, the Monument and the Resting Place

In addition, Arlington, as a national cemetery, is also the final resting place for freed slaves, Supreme Court Justices, Presidents, and other prominent individuals. Nineteen American astronauts are buried in Arlington as well, including the crew of the space shuttle Challenger, which exploded moments after lift off in 1986.

However, to veterans, Arlington is regarded first and foremost as a military cemetery. While all these grounds are hallowed there is one unique place in Arlington which holds a special meaning to every veteran. Known as the "Tomb of the Unknowns" or the "Tomb of the Unknown Soldier," this revered symbol of sacrifice is guarded 24 hours a day regardless of weather. It honors three veterans who lost their lives serving their nation, whose remains could never be identified and were lost to their families. The simple inscription reads: "Here Rests In Honored Glory An American Soldier Known But To God." The tomb of these veterans stands as a sacred monument to all who served, especially those who lie buried in anonymous graves in distant lands and those honored patriots whose remains were given to time and history.

From the courageous men and women who served their country in uniform to surgeons and poets; explorers and statesmen to Medal of Honor recipients; Revolutionary War combatants to present day casualties; this hallowed ground is an enduring reminder of heroic sacrifice, and in the air over each of those graves the simple notes of *Taps* echo proudly, honoring all who served.

HERE RESTS IN
HONORED GLORY

AN AMERICAN
SOLDIER

KNOWN BUT TO GOD

★
___

Arlington National Cemetery

"These are hallowed grounds"

Veterans Day & Flag Day
Origins and Symbols

November 11, 1918, what became known as "Armistice Day", recognizing the end of World War I fighting, became official in America in 1926 through a Congressional resolution. It became a national holiday in 1938 by similar Congressional action. But only a few years after "the War to end all wars" ended, war again broke out in Europe. Sixteen and a half million Americans took part. Four hundred seven thousand of them died in service, more than 292,000 in battle.

In 1947, Raymond Weeks, a World War II veteran, organized "National Veterans Day," which included a parade and other festivities to honor all veterans. The event was held on November 11, then designated Armistice Day. In 1954, Congress passed the bill proclaiming November 11 as Veterans Day. In 1982, Weeks received the Presidential Citizens Medal from President Ronald Reagan. Weeks's local parade and ceremonies are now an annual event celebrated nationwide.

At 11 a.m. each November 11, a color guard representing all military services executes "Present Arms" at the Tomb of the Unknown Soldier in Arlington National Cemetery. The nation's tribute to its war dead is also symbolized by the laying of a presidential wreath as a bugler plays *Taps*. Chaired by the Secretary of Veterans Affairs, Veterans Day ceremonies at Arlington and elsewhere are coordinated by the President's Veterans Day National Committee, which represents national veterans organizations. Governors of many states and U.S. territories also appoint Veterans Day chairpersons who, in cooperation with the National Committee and the Department of Defense, arrange and promote local ceremonies.

Memorial Day

A National Tribute

We remember those who died in service to their country on Memorial Day. As long as loved ones have been lost to battle, days have been set aside to honor them. In Civil War times communities all over the country remembered their fallen townsfolk as Memorial Day was unofficially celebrated at different times and in different ways in every region.

May 15, 1868, General John Logan, National Commander of the Grand Army of the Republic, officially proclaimed Memorial Day as flowers were placed on the graves of Union and Confederate soldiers in Arlington Cemetery. After World War I, the nation had a day of remembrance for those who had given their lives in the armed services. With the National Holiday Act of 1971, the last Monday in May became the official day, ensuring a long weekend as a federal holiday.

The Thursday preceding Memorial Day, soldiers of the 3rd U.S. Infantry place small American flags at over 260,000 graves in Arlington National Cemetery. They keep watch every hour of the weekend to make sure each flag stands. All over the nation families stand in silence above graves with fresh flowers to honor citizens whose service has kept us free. The secularization of the day as little more than a "long weekend" has weakened its hold on the American mind. Many would like to see the observance returned to May 30, the original day of remembrance.

In 2000 Congress passed a resolution called the National Moment of Remembrance, so that all Americans at 3:00 p.m. on Memorial Day might pause to remember those who died for our nation. Let us turn from the "vacation" frame of mind on Memorial Day long enough to acknowledge the greatest contribution one can give to the United States, the gift of one's life.

Paying Tribute . . .

To Grieve ...

Mourning One Who Served

A Voice for the Sorrow. To mourn our lost loved ones is to acknowledge their place in our hearts. It is to give a voice to the sorrow that permeates our souls. It is to recognize that in some ways we are truly diminished by death. And in that acknowledgement, in the tenor of the voice and the manner of the recognition, we become ever more human as we are connected to all those others who must come to the same place of emptiness and choose to go another day.

In our mourning we give ourselves to others, to help and be helped. In our mourning we give ourselves to the great whirlwind of sadness and joy, loss and gain that is the human experience. And though we are diminished, we are also increased by the love of those around us. Military forces have always bonded fiercely through the deaths of fellow compatriots and they know a union makes them stronger as a result.

In this section, we seek to give that voice to your sorrow by setting forth some of the accumulated wisdom concerning loss and grief. But your grief is yours and the voice of your sorrow is a voice we hear and a voice we honor.

★

Healing the Heart

"The heart has its reasons which reason does not know."

Blaise Pascal

The ancient truth: "Time is the greatest physician" is of little consolation when we have just lost a loved one. Broken hearts are not mended like broken fences. Grief is not a project, but a process. A great writer once said, "Life is not a problem to be solved but a mystery to be lived." And so it is with our grieving. We must somehow learn to live the mystery of it, for our balm is life itself. And the heart is bound to take us places we did not expect to journey. Perhaps the most we can do is learn to trust the heart's own reasons, which reason does not know. The heart is like a wounded animal seeking refuge. It seeks a place to find its own healing powers and its boundaries are built of love and faith, of memory and friendship.

Some years ago Dr. Elisabeth Kübler-Ross, through interviews with the terminally ill, found paths the human heart seems to commonly travel, with much individual variation of course, when confronted with great loss. What she found fit so well the emotional struggles of so many, that her model or "stages" of grief have since provided grieving people a kind of map of their own sorrow. The stages do not treat grief as a "problem to be solved," but rather as a "mystery to be lived." They track our grief in a way that can be of great aid and comfort. For this reason we present here a brief overview of these stages in the hopes that you or your family members might better understand how very human your responses to great loss are. It is our hope as well that, though you are changed forever by your loss, you can go on to live your life fully and with inspiration, meaning and love.

Grieving in Stages

In times gone by, common sense told us things about ourselves that modern scholarship is just now beginning to verify scientifically. Modern science tells us, for instance, that grieving over the death or illness of one close to us is a "natural" process. Psychologists tell us that one of the more important elements in healthy grieving is having a belief system that gives meaning to suffering and death. We know that suffering and death not only have meaning but are at the core of our understanding and experience of life itself. Life teaches us that enduring the inevitable trials of our existence is to somehow transcend it.

Rites of burial and funeral proceedings down through the ages have recognized the needs of the bereaved. But as cultures and societies change, so do some of our expressions of belief about death. In the fast pace of modern "mobile" society we sometimes forget how the comfort of memorial observance united us in ways that made our suffering more bearable and the pangs of loss less devastating.

Reliance upon our friends and family does not eliminate our pain over the loss of a loved one. But their comfort and love can infuse our suffering with meaning. Our natural longing to be with a loved one who has passed away, or our longing to have them return to us is a model of how we should strive for goodness and kindness in our lives. Our deceased loved ones remain in our hearts just as goodness dwells within us. We will still undergo the natural stages of grief that have been described so well in recent years. But behind each grief-stricken instinct is the knowledge that death is not in vain, but rather that our suffering, our grief, will find objective meaning in the time to come, specifically in our relationships with those around us.

Denial

What the terminally ill patient experienced was the grief attendant to his/her own imminent death. And we have found through observation that the same kinds of things are experienced by those grieving the loss of a loved one.

★

───────

The circumstances surrounding the death of a loved one tremendously affect the way in which the family deals with their loss. The sudden and tragic death of a child elicits a different response than the expected passing of a grandparent who has led a long and productive life. The loss of one currently in military service carries its own particular depth of sorrow and grief. Death, in and of itself, holds the power to strike at our hearts and cause us to recoil in disbelief. In fact, a common immediate response to news of the death of a loved one is denial. Denial is a natural human response which helps to shield us from the emotional devastation that can come from tragic and/or sorrowful news. It would be common, for instance, to hear a widow say, upon hearing of the death of her husband in the service, "I know he is gone, but I just can't fully believe that he won't be coming home from overseas. I keep waiting to see him, for his deployment to end, for him to play baseball in the back yard with our son like he used to." Losing someone so dear is literally unbelievable. Gradually, however, the reality of death sinks in; but that reality is or can be mitigated by our commitment to pass on the positive lessons of the life that just left us.

 ## Anger

It is also quite normal for the grieving family to feel anger over the loss of their dear one. With whom are we angry? At our loved one for leaving us? But that's not being fair to the memory of the deceased, is it? Well, maybe we are being too hard on ourselves. With whom are we usually the angriest—isn't it someone near and dear to us? Temporary anger is a natural part of the process. In this light, even anger at the deceased is understandable and completely human.

Perhaps we are angry at the prospect of death itself. Sometimes it seems so terribly unfair, so randomly destructive, so wantonly mad. How can it be that children of loving parents are suddenly orphaned because of a tragic event no one can explain? How can it be that such good people die so young, before their mark is fully made, before their love felt widely enough? Perhaps there is an enemy in a foreign land, an enemy we cannot see, one who has killed with a perverse righteousness and fervor and we cannot see this enemy's face and we want to know why this enemy hates us so. How can it be that one of us must travel the rest of this sometimes rutted road alone, without the usual aid and comfort of a life companion? Indeed there are so many questions death poses to us. And it can be an excruciating realization that to so many of these questions the simple answer is: *We just don't know.*

But we will eventually know if our anger is left unexpressed or unattended to, for it will resurface in ways that can be most unhealthy. First, we must recognize the anger that tears away at us and know that it is a natural feeling that can, if channeled wisely, help us walk through the stages of grief to wholeness. Knowing and accepting our anger for what it is, a natural and temporary coping mechanism, is essential to the grief process. Denying our anger ensures its eventual return on a more destructive level; whereas, discussing our feelings with a spiritual advisor or a counselor can help us get beyond it. Perhaps we will try taking our anger to an understanding friend or professional, a veterans group or others in bereavement. We certainly need not be alone with such charged emotion. For those who have walked our path may understand us in a way few others can.

Bargaining

Terminally ill patients reach a point where they instinctively, out of the will to live, begin to bargain, usually with the God of their understanding. The plea may be "If only you would save me, . . ." The family of the dying patient wishes to make similar deals — it is a desperate (but so very human) effort to change what we cannot. This bargaining stage infiltrates the grieving process in that we may begin to make demands upon those around us because we feel we've been cheated of our loved one's presence. The cold realization that we cannot bargain our loved one back into existence; that we cannot wake from this dream wherein life has been altered so drastically for us is too much to handle. So the tendency to try to make a deal, with God, with Life, with people such as doctors, friends, in the case of a veteran perhaps even the government, etc. is a natural outgrowth of denial. The logic of the principle of cause and effect now seems completely illogical. We may think: "I have tried my best to live well, why then is my family being subjected to this emotionally devastating series of events? Why is this happening to me and to my family? I seem to be able to fix other things in my life, why can't I fix this? If I could only do these certain things or behave in this certain way, won't the pain of my loved one's death go away? Won't everything just be different when I wake up one morning?"

Sometimes we may decide to go to great lengths to force changes in our lives for which we may not be ready. We do so in an effort to alleviate the great loss we have suffered. But in the end the only bargain is living through what we are meant to live through. Then and only then will we know the natural and gradual release from the deep sorrow that has so overtaken us now.

And along the way we will usually find friends and other loved ones who really do know the depths to which our bereavement can take us. And even as we bargain, or try to make deals, love deepens and begins to see us through.

Depression

As our denial and anger subside, and as our notion of what we can change and what we cannot becomes clearer, a powerful and real sense of loss can overwhelm us. We become engulfed in memories of the life we led with our dearly departed loved one. We find it hard to muster any energy or respond with any sense of enthusiasm to the many kindnesses shown us. Our sadness becomes even heavier.

People have described depression in many ways. Some say it is frozen anger. The anger that has not been channeled appropriately or assimilated in a healthy way remains to wreak havoc in our hearts. Some say in depression it feels like we are just shutting down, that we are withdrawing from life itself, closing the doors to our soul that once welcomed in positive thoughts and ideas, as well as people close to us. Some say depression keeps one from focusing on any direction, like a traveler on a traffic circle who keeps turning down streets only to find dead ends. Despair lurks in the shadows and the world closes in. Depression can be frightful and crippling. And we would do well to recognize its destructive power.

Yet it is during this phase of grief, this depression, that love can enter our lives in a much deeper way, for it is during this heart-breaking time that we instinctively and most humbly cry out, and, in so doing, begin to tap into our innermost strengths. But the crying out is key. We need never resist the natural need to share ourselves with someone close, be it a friend or even a professional counselor. Depression is but a normal manifestation of deep mourning, a natural phase of the grieving process that will pass in time, in healthy interaction with our family and friends and with an intimate connection to the deepest part of ourselves wherein we find a strength we perhaps never knew existed.

Acceptance

If, with help, we experience these various phases of grief, but keep from becoming frozen in any one of them, then we naturally begin to accept the death of our dearly departed. Our acceptance is drenched in pain, for we have loved strongly; it is covered with sorrow, for we have given our heart and received the heart of another; it is riddled with remorse, for we feel the agonizing incision of loss; and yet we accept.

Somehow we have learned to keep on living. Maybe it was a trusted friend who helped see us through the toughest moments. Maybe it was a veteran or family member of a veteran keenly aware of our loss and able to understand like few others. Maybe it was a spiritual life we tapped into that gave us comfort. Perhaps our survival instincts came together to fashion a new way of living, living with loss but also with the joy and the peace that a good life offers. We must keep in mind that any stage of grief may return in a less intense form, and we must be prepared to cope, having learned much about living with loss in the last few months. But as each episode occurs, we feel a bit stronger, a bit more able to endure. And endure we do, by taking what we have learned and reaching out to another human being.

We begin to live with the hurt, to interpret our suffering in light of what we can do to ease the suffering of others. We draw nearer to those who offer their love genuinely. We reach out, we remember, we pay homage, we love, we carry on.

★

Grief

The Individual Experience

Just as every life is an individual life, so is every experience of the loss of a loved one an individual experience. Each bereaved person filters the experience of grief through their own personality and through their own ways of coping. Each person brings their particular belief system to bear on the matters at hand. And this is as it should be. But the individual's personality, experience and beliefs are not the only variables in the grieving process. Who passed away and the way they passed is also a most important determinant of how we experience grief.

Living with the sorrow that accompanies the death of a loved one is always difficult. But because each type of relationship with each different loved one is unique, we may feel very different feelings as we journey through our grief. The following section takes a look at various expressions of grief based upon who has passed away. It is not inclusive of every situation but is meant rather to empathize with you in whatever situation you find yourself, whether as a widow, a bereaved parent, a saddened grandchild, etc.

The circumstances of our loved one's passing are also important variables that influence our grief. A sudden death, a long illness, a unique circumstance, the particularly incisive grief associated with a combat death, all these factors have much to do with how we encounter bereavement.

Just as you bring your own individuality to the place of sorrow, you also bring that individuality to the "living through" process, the same individual strength that has seen you through many other of life's trials. In this section it is our hope to tap into that very personal strength as we reflect on grief itself and the sometimes hidden power of the human spirit.

The Loss of a Spouse

With the death of your spouse, a huge part of yourself is gone now, too. The grief is palpable and your best friend and confidant is not there. Those widowed know a loneliness others can't imagine. How is it possible to go on alone? The grief is immediate and intimate and cannot be explained; only lived through with care and respect. Feelings of betrayal may come. "How can I be left alone like this?" The spouses of those who served have most likely faced this unique fear. But nothing prepares one adequately for such loss.

Military families may undergo a special kind of grief associated with war and its attendant casualties. A spouse in such a situation may feel hatred for an enemy that delivered this seemingly unbearable blow, only to find that wholesale hatred brings no emotional satisfaction or hope to the aching heart. Often the military itself does much to offer solace and many military families join together when death and love of country become one.

Just as grief is a process, so is learning to live again. Recovery becomes almost a form of art in that living through the grief is a very conscious effort. Acceptance of the death of a spouse and a subsequent new way of life, with a corresponding new identity does not just happen. It is crafted with the help of those who understand and those who love you. Opening one's heart to help can call for the same kind of courage the one who served was called upon to muster at some point in military life. Life will go on and you will find reason and purpose once more, but these adjustments take place at your own pace. There are a growing number of widow/widower support groups that can be of great help. However you find your way, you will realize that your experience can help other people. It may be through your witness of strength or your quiet understanding of another family member's pain. It may be in your relationships with other veterans' families or perhaps in some way you never suspected. Though the memory of your spouse is intact, somehow a commitment to keeping on, alive and hopeful, proves that even a broken heart can grow larger.

The Loss of a Parent

Someone once said that parents stand between us and mortality. After the death of a parent we come to understand a little better how swift the journey really is. The death may come as an overdue blessing or an unexpected trauma; therefore each death dictates to some extent the tenor of the accompanying grief. We may have lived far away, or we may have had to play the role of caregiver to one or both of our parents in their later years. We may regret the emotional baggage we left. We may find ourselves struggling with forgiveness. We are surprised at the long buried memories that surface, some perhaps sweet, some perhaps not so. We may have to attend closely to a surviving parent and feel our own grief being suppressed by the obligations of the time.

Our experience in a military family can also help shape the contours of our grief in ways that only military families fully understand. The moving about in early life, for instance, may have had effects that resurface now. And of course if their passing is as a result of military service then deep and unsettling issues can certainly come to the fore. But regardless of circumstances, pride in a parent's service can be a soothing balm during difficult times.

These are only some of the possibilities that we may encounter. We carry a deep emotional connection to our mothers and fathers that death does not destroy. Whatever the circumstances, there must come a time of healing. The connection to our parents is not lost, it is changed and in the changing, it becomes more uniquely ours. It is this continuing bond that determines the way we keep their memory alive. Perhaps with our own children, we tell stories of the past and recollect meaningful or fun times. Parents who were veterans may have had stories of far away places, of courage in the midst of fear. By passing their stories on we help create the images of our parents that our own children will carry with them. We may also discover our siblings in a new light. We empathize with them in ways others could not. We might seek the solace that friends or neighbors can provide. We may be surprised at the impact of our loss. It is a time for gentleness and healing. We listen to our own hearts and we forgive. We listen to our own hearts and we share what we have heard with someone, now or later, who we know is feeling what we have felt. And we learn that, through it all, love is always the answer.

The Loss of a Child

What loss can be greater than the loss of one's child? The passing of one's offspring brings with it a sense of diminishment as in perhaps no other way, for our sons and daughters are meant to live on past the course of our own lives. The lives of our children are supposed to stretch out beyond our years and give us the satisfaction of watching the marvelous handiwork of humanity unfold before us in the beauty and wonderment of their own families. So how can so tragic a thing as this be? The efforts of finite minds cannot but fall short of understanding.

If our son or daughter was in the service we are certainly afforded the satisfaction that they sacrificed for their country. We know a patriot's heart is a noble heart and we are gratified by the response of their fellows in the military, where friendships take on a fervor and allegiance second to none.

We trudge through this great sorrow sometimes an hour at a time and we may feel as if we live in slow motion. The rituals we have enacted for other deaths in the family, such as the visit to the graveside, the keeping of a photograph album or the telling of stories about the deceased now are even more painful, but no less necessary to the grieving process. Some families have found solace in the establishment of funds or memorials that pertain to the life of their son or daughter. Gestures of this kind are anything but empty. They can resonate for years to come in positive ways for family members.

Love slowly embraces our torn hearts and begins the long and difficult road to acceptance. We may find ourselves avoiding friends to keep from breaking down. Our sorrow may be unimaginably intense. But we must hear with our hearts in this distressed time, for there are others who have experienced something akin to our pain and we may need to seek their presence if not their counsel. Ask your funeral director, pastor, neighbors or the Department of Veterans Affairs if they know of support groups addressing this particular kind of loss. There is a growing awareness of the efficacy of such groups. In time, because our child's heart has become so deeply embodied in our own, we are able to help someone else whose sorrow and loneliness is all but overwhelming. And in that moment our son or our daughter has come to life in a new and unique way.

The Loss of a Sibling

When a sibling passes away we sometimes find ourselves returning to the days of childhood, not only in memory but also, to a certain degree, in our emotional lives. We feel a sense of unfairness when a younger sibling dies and with one older we may have a sense of loss similar to the losing of a parent. Family dynamics are always in some state of flux, but this wound affects the whole system of family relationships. One sibling may have been the peacemaker in the family, another the main caretaker in regard to parents. A death among siblings can shake the foundation of these established roles. Some siblings have stayed closer over the years than others and these brothers or sisters may now have to look to others for support and comfort.

Obviously, this is a time when families can demonstrate their unity or renew a unity that may once have existed. If the sibling was in the service there may be very difficult extenuating circumstances the family has to deal with. Often weakened family ties have been strengthened by the shared grief and struggles attendant to a sibling's death. And within every family there will also arise the pockets of loneliness that must be attended to. In honor of the deceased, new and helpful alliances may form that actually give strength to individual family members.

But it should not be surprising or considered in any way disloyal to feel the need for counsel from outside the family. Friends from church, veterans groups, work or the community may be better confidants than family members with whom we have had little close contact. Nor should we be surprised if "childlike" feelings re-emerge as we grieve our brother or sister's passing. Reason must recognize these feelings for what they are. The child inside of us is demanding attention. But remember, it is the adult who tends to the childlike feelings, therefore we do so with care and with a respect for what once existed in the life of our family. And in this way, we truly honor the memory of a brother or sister who has gone on.

The Loss of a Special Relative

We have all had those relatives who have captured our hearts over the years. It might have been an uncle who had a knack for entertaining kids, an aunt whose cookies and stories we will never forget or a cousin who was more like a sibling. It could have been a service member whose life conjured for us adventure and intrigue or the lure of far away places.

There was just something special about our relationship that we both knew and felt: a similar outlook, a shared way of seeing things. We enjoyed talking about the peculiarities of our extended family. We may have shared how we each differed from our respective immediate families, a sharing which formed a bond stronger than many familial bonds.

The void left when a special relative passes away is mightily felt and difficult to endure. Few may understand how deep the connection had been, how strong the bond. So where do we go for comfort? With whom may we now speak of this special friendship? Does anyone understand? Those who have now, or have had in the past, the same kind of relationship with a special relative certainly understand. They know how endearing a familial friendship can be. At some point we begin to observe closely our family members who we think may indeed have such a relationship. Sometimes we feel these relationships are few and far between, but perhaps there are more of them out there than we may have thought at first.

We go through the grieving stages, we talk to others and we even seek similar relationships with other family members to varying degrees of success. But the bottom line is that we will always have a special place in our hearts for these special relatives, and no coping mechanism will take that away. Our special relative is and will always be, missed sorely. We live with them inside of us, their spirit helping animate us along our way, their memory forever cherished.

The Loss of a Grandparent

Unfortunately, modern society evidences a remarkable lack of respect with regard to the dignity of older people. So as we participate in the arrangements of our grandparent's funeral we are forced to review the difficulties he or she encountered in the process of aging in modern times. We may feel guilty for our own lack of participation in this unique life. Perhaps we have lived away and lost some of the emotional connection we once had. Perhaps our grandparent had moved on to a nursing home, had dealt with a series of sad declines in health or had gone down hill after the death of their own spouse. These are realities of modern life and death for the aged. We may also begin to remember a childhood in which our grandparents played a role. Perhaps we've idealized this time and now long for the warmth, security and simplicity of another time and place. We begin to wonder about our own "golden" years.

Even if we are relieved that our loved one no longer suffers, it is wise not to underestimate the impact of this loss. Something of ourselves has passed, too and this may be the first time we encounter deep loss on life's terms. Grieving a grandparent can move us to a greater sensitivity to the burdens all families carry. Grief can make us more present for anyone struggling to accept the demise of a dear loved one. We seek the solace of family, of contacts among clergy or understanding friends. We gather photographs as we gather memories, and we thereby recognize the human dignity of grandma or grandpa, a dignity modern life may have been remiss in seeing.

And if our grandparent was one who served, perhaps it is time to investigate our own history by looking at the military service records. The last known veteran of World War I died just recently and our World War II veterans are leaving us every day. These are folks that served in a frightening time and it is befitting to honor that service. Perhaps some of the information contained in this volume could help you become more aware of this service. Medals or records that may have been lost might now be readily attainable. You may decide to review or even collect the military memorabilia that was a tribute to your grandparent's service to country. You learn of a patriotism seldom witnessed today. Ultimately, you come back to a kind of deep and abiding love learned generations ago in the life of your family. It is a loyalty and respect that will surely endure.

The Loss of a Close Friend

What is it that makes up the special quality of a close friendship? Is it shared experiences or similar ideals? Perhaps we crossed paths at work or in our social or family life. Perhaps service to our country or even combat brought us together in a unique way. A close friend seems to know us like a brother or a sister would know us. Somewhere along the line this friend was there when support, comfort or help of any kind was needed. Close friendships make for hard good-byes. We know we never matched their generosity though others tell us we did. We know we will miss them differently than family, but in a way that stings deeply. This friend may have been a special link to meaningful memories or profound experiences of the past, or a refreshing surprise of our later years. The friendship may have been there for decades or have just begun its development. It may be a remnant of military service together, hard times endured and joy found in unlikely places. It was sustained by concern and thoughtfulness, and the loss has wounded us deeply.

Where do we go for consolation? After all, it was so often this very friend who supplied that consolation. This is a time to understand the nature of friendship and reflect upon it. We may never find another friend as good, but we may express the special qualities of our friendship with others. More deep and abiding friendships exist among people than we might think. At some point in the midst of this unique manifestation of sorrow, we might want to talk about the things that made the friendship what it was.

Maybe we become a beacon for the lonely, for those who need a connection to other people that has somehow passed them by. We know what a healthy reliance upon friendship can mean. Perhaps we know of service men and women who have lost friends or family members. Maybe there is an old one whose friends have all passed on. Our experience may just touch one like this in a special way, for surely our friendship touched us in ways we will remember fondly for some time to come.

★

How We Lost Them

The manner in which a loved one has passed away has everything to do with the kind of grief we subsequently experience. The various stages of grief represent commonly shared ways of coping with great loss, but the particular context of that loss also affects us in highly individual ways. Here we briefly examine ways of coping with our loss depending upon the circumstances of the demise of our loved one. Of course there is something uniquely personal in all experiences of grief. But however the death has occurred, we may discover threads of empathy when we open our hearts to others who have been wounded by the loss of one dear to them.

A Distant Light

When one we care about is at death's door, we instinctively go to them. And yet, there are times when situations prevent our being there. Perhaps we live across the country and cannot get to the bedside in time; perhaps the death is as a result of a sudden tragedy and we are unable to be with family and friends for the funeral; perhaps the special circumstances military families commonly encounter such as the tragedies of war keep us from being present. The distance, for any reason, seems unbearable. Indeed, not being present goes against our instincts and can wreak havoc with us emotionally.

Where do we turn and what do we do? We turn to friends, counselors, veterans groups, clergy or other understanding people who can empathize with us. We don't keep it all inside, just adding to our sense of isolation. We cope by memorializing the one we have lost. We do this by remembering our connection, maybe even in journal form or in letters or other communications to family. We might talk to those who were present and share with them the same kinds of things we would have shared if we had been able to attend. We try to break the distance down, even a little, through communication and long distance care. What do we do? We cherish the memory of our loved one. Love and memory have no physical bounds; they travel the world and touch far away hearts. And a love that is shared can be a distant light that may just help someone lost in sorrow find their way back to life.

★

A Natural Course

Medical technology has not only made astounding progress in battling the effects of many once debilitating and fatal diseases, it has also extended our life spans considerably in the last fifty years. This wonderful progress, however, has sometimes created bewildering end of life issues. When once an elder may have died of what was called "natural causes" most likely in their own home, today the hospital has become the common locale of the passing of our family members and friends. Quite often last days are spent in a painless, but drug clouded haze of medical machinery in an institutional atmosphere. This all too common set of circumstances makes it all the more important to bring to the death of a loved one a sense of human dignity, a realization that even the pain of living and of dying has redeeming qualities that live on in loved ones.

And when one we love has lived long and the natural course of events has escorted them to life's end, we must look beyond the unnatural departure modern society has created and give thanks for a long life, perhaps one that allowed for a wisdom and bearing only years and service to one's country and family can bring, perhaps for the experience of grandchildren in one's life and other joys that are possible in the golden years.

We realize that our gratitude for the life of an elder who has passed will be noticed by the younger members of the family. To plant with them the seed that says cherish life in all its forms is an invaluable gift to enjoy, even in the midst of sorrow and grief.

A Special Circumstance

There are some tragedies in life that bear with them an added hurt. Whether the pain is due to controversy, violence, despair or other confounding circumstances, it can be extremely intense and unsettling. Sometimes the death of a loved one carries this added weight, and so too do we carry the weight in our grief. The violence in our schoolyards, the stinging tears of heartbreak over a suicide, the devastation Nature herself sometimes unleashes, the pure sadness associated with a stillbirth or miscarriage, the particularly ravaging pain of the casualties of war, all of these special circumstances and more bring with them a burden beyond the grief itself.

As every situation is unique, so is every manifestation of sorrow. With any set of special circumstances, anger may plague the family or friends in grief. We may be angry at society for its insensitivity to the situation, at friends for not understanding, at ourselves for what we perceive we might have been able to do and even at the deceased for leaving us in such a fashion. It may also be at a foreign enemy for their misguided ferocity and hatred. These forms of anger are common and may perhaps play a larger role in the grieving process when special circumstances are present. Special circumstances can also bring a sense of irrational guilt. We imagine some solution we could have brought about but did not, when reason would tell us otherwise.

There is no "solution" to living with the grief of a death that has occurred as a result of a special circumstance. The human heart is embattled and we incur the wounds. This is a time, however, when helpful professionals may come to our aid, for the maze of sad bewilderment can lead to great depression. It is essential to cry out for help to the people we trust, and perhaps even to professionals who have dealt with these matters before. Support groups have been of great help to many in such difficult times. We know we must live in the maze of this mystery, but we must also find a way to eventually return to the peace and even the joy we deserve as a member of the human family. We must be gentle with ourselves; it is a time of great care.

A Sudden Blow

Death is rarely welcomed, but it is many times expected. It may be because of a serious illness evident in our loved one's life or the natural course of time. Families sometimes see warning signs, especially in the case of the older members. But sometimes death comes as a complete and jolting surprise. Perhaps a young person in the prime of life is suddenly struck down or a tragedy of inestimable proportion wounds a family and its friends as deeply as one may be wounded. Military families face this circumstance more than most. The shock of such a death is a part of the grieving process that may not be present with another kind of death. Everything remains shrouded in mystery. For loved ones there is little to hold onto except each other. With sudden tragedies families learn to put aside differences and bond together, using each other's strength as perhaps an only defense against the pain of such profound sorrow.

But we still must find a way to cope. There may have been many things left unsaid, hurdles left yet to the relationship with the deceased. Where do we take this residue of uncertainty and agony? We search our spiritual lives for the help we need and the results of that search direct us onward. We search our hearts for some manner of expressing the void left in our life. We look for help in family friends, clergy and professionals. We read, we pray, we talk, we listen.

There is no way around heart break. But after a broken heart can come a sense of what others have felt before us and what some others are yet to know. We may end up being a refuge for these dear souls, a true refuge because we understand this special wound and we have become willing to hold another's hand as they walk through it.

A Vigil Kept

When a protracted illness envelops the life of a family and their friends, the wear on each human spirit can sometimes be devastating. Forbearance is a virtue that certainly comes into play and is the challenge of each individual who becomes a caregiver in such a situation. To witness death in slow motion can be practically unbearable. But somehow, we do it anyway; we stay the course and give what aid we can, learning the hard way that death can be the height of mercy and peace.

Sometimes long illnesses can be financially overwhelming for a family. Many times a financial advisor can be of help when the medical or nursing care bills are growing. There are an increasing number of professionals specializing in these areas today. This may well be a time to look at possible financial options. A long illness can also be physically and emotionally wearing upon family and friends. Having someone to talk with about what the family is going through is paramount. This may be a professional in such matters such as a psychologist or other counselor; it may be a member of the clergy trained to help with human problems that manifest their spiritual nature or it may be a caring friend in whom we have great confidence.

One thing we found in this painful process was how to recognize the special moments when our loved one either consciously or unconsciously taught us great lessons. It may have been a special gesture to a child, a small utterance of wisdom about the past life of the family, a forgiving nod or perhaps a glance that seemed to come from another world. We may or may not have had those special moments with our loved one. If we have, we cherish them; if not we still know that our vigil kept, somehow in the big picture of things, was good and right and giving. And we learn that, as difficult as suffering is, it does have meaning and will continue to be one of the foundations for goodness in our lives.

To Carry On ...

Continuing to Live

The Great Decision. To carry on after the death of a loved one is the result of a decision. It is a decision made after we've traveled the stages of grief and arrived at a place of acceptance. It is a decision of consequence and import. It is a decision we may have to make more than once or even on a regular basis, a thousand times over. But it is a decision we make nonetheless. It is the decision to live. We may have made it intellectually some time ago. But at some point we make the decision on a gut level. We decide to live on, many times because we know our loved one would have it no other way. We also make a decision, either consciously or subconsciously, about how we are going to continue to live. Will we sit in a room and watch the walls close in or will we go before our family and friends, offering what hope we can by our example and what consolation we can by our experience? We make the great decision to live and like in the last lines of the great Robert Frost poem, *Stopping By Woods on a Snowy Evening*, we realize that:

> The woods are lovely, dark and deep.
> But I have promises to keep,
> And miles to go before I sleep,
> And miles to go before I sleep.

★

The Year to Come

A Summary of the First Difficult Year

Each season seems to touch us in unique ways when we are enduring great sorrow. Rather than being dulled by grief, our senses are almost
painfully alive. Be it winter, spring, summer or fall, the character of the
season enters into our affliction. The leafless trees of winter stand only for
our loneliness and even spring bursts with a life we do not feel. Summer's
ease eludes us and the chill of fall reminds us of endings and our own loss.
And in each season is a holiday we recall experiencing with our loved one.
Some are worse than others. Thanksgiving and Christmas can be especially
hard. Birthdays and anniversaries of any season sting with longing. We may
reach deep into our souls for answers that don't ever seem to come. The
heat is burdensome and the cold a copious weight. In our innermost selves

we cry out for relief, almost fearful of leaving our grief, for we are not the same now and responding to the world around us again is almost like a betrayal of our loved one. Going it alone is unimaginable.

Yet it may just be that somewhere in this visceral crying out faint surprises begin to appear. We may notice like never before the delightfully enchanting demeanor of a child. Perhaps we are touched in a special way by some common act of kindness or compassion. We may even feel the distinctively expressive, bittersweet magnetism of a brilliant sunset or a vigorous rainfall. All these experiences are flavored with our own sadness yet, as we are alive to our own pain, so do we become more aware of the sufferings of others. And so also do we begin to feel more acutely the kindnesses shown to us by others. Because we have been touched by great anguish, somehow we become more vulnerable to live encounters with mercy, grace, patience and empathy. Symbolically, (and slowly) we learn to open the window and breathe in the fragrance of the season. Perhaps we begin only to appease a friend or family member, nevertheless we begin. We walk outside into the season's peculiar air. Senses heightened by heartache reach out to engage the world again, leaf by raindrop by ray of morning light. And ever so slowly we see, smell, hear, taste and touch the people, places and things of life. We experience everything in its season: the diminished pace of summertime, the brisk wistfulness of autumn, the stark invigoration of winter and the rejuvenation of the spring. We become a part of the seasons and are affected by them in new ways because we are new.

Each time of year asks of us a new kind of strength and we respond by revealing a fortitude we didn't really know was there. The courage of a veteran hides in our own heart. We have not given up missing our loved ones; we have accommodated our woundedness. We have not stopped loving; we have opened an afflicted heart to healing. We have not forgotten; we have learned to make more memories. Let us here walk through the seasons, meditating on the profound beauty of creation, grateful for the loved ones we have known and served with our strength, loyalty and love. We are forever changed by our loss; more vulnerable yet somehow stronger. We bear our crosses with dignity and, as the seasons change, so do our hearts inevitably anticipate the days of life to come.

★

Summer

Old and New Paths Merge

This season harkens back to childhood days when school let out, shoes came off and kids went exploring in the pleasant idleness youth affords. Of course we cannot recapture those days and that time, but we can appreciate the time of year with a more childlike acceptance of the losses we have endured and the triumphs we have enjoyed. The emotional hardship that grief presents can be as draining as the lingering heat of summer. It sometimes seems that all the energy we have has been expelled just to keep going. A cool breeze, a slice of shade or even a bit of recreation would be just the thing to provide a little relief and regeneration. Psychologically, it is incumbent upon us as we travel through our grief, to find the respite that comes from some time off, a little shade, a cool breeze or a touch of child-like activity, just as those who served had their passes and their furloughs. The time off may be vacation or just a visit to another place; the breeze could be a friend who is a "breath of fresh air"; the shade may be an activity like a church group, social or veterans' club or any other group of people with whom we look forward to meeting. And the recreation may be simple neighborhood walks or even a structured activity that gets the blood flowing. All of us, bereaved or not, need regular stress reducing, spiritually affirming experiences in the presence of people with whom we feel comfortable.

MEDITATION

This season we will attempt to see certain things with childlike eyes. There is an essential innocence in all of us that only needs tapping in order to make us more complete, with strength for our difficulties and direction for our joys. Let us consciously look for ways to find fellowship with people. Let us look for the cool breeze and the carpet of shade that give relief from the long days of summer as well as the stress-reducing activities that help to counteract the weariness of sorrow. Let us find ways to relax a little and find time for leisure and good health.

Autumn

A Colorful Exchange

Fall comes in with its own unique sensations. The clean, crisp air fills us with welcome relief from the summer's heat and thoughts that naturally seem to journey back to days gone by. Sometimes a melancholy comes over us, a longing for the people and situations that used to give us such joy. There is certainly nothing unnatural about these thoughts. We let them come and go. We let nature affect us without succumbing to overriding sadness or depression. We allow nature to run her course through us in peace and understanding.

With the changing of the leaves we tend to reflect upon the changes we have undergone and are still experiencing. Even in the midst of so many changes, nature flaunts her radiance just as memories of our loved one still glitter in the dusk of each day. We recall the triumphs of the human spirit we witnessed in the life of our loved one. And even as we hear the call of *Taps* in our mind and our heart, we still appreciate the luminous, colorful moments that have enriched our lives and that continue to do so.

MEDITATION

This season we will observe the constancy of nature as we appreciate the joys of yesterday and the hope for tomorrow. Our hearts will go out to other grieving families, especially the families of those who served. We will let Mother Nature speak gently and with her abounding wisdom. We will venture out into the freshness of a new season. We will accept the inevitability of recurring sadness just as we cultivate hope and the promise of new and better days ahead.

This fall we will purposefully call to mind the victories life has allowed us and all our loved ones whether associated with military life or not. There have been some very good times, most associated with overcoming obstacles life put in our path. And there are victories yet left to experience. The campaign is not over, so we keep our eyes open to be of witness to the bright and enduring power of the human spirit.

Winter

A Time for Reflection

In the gray cloud cover of winter, the cold night air and the once green trees now barren, we see how nature can visually represent the depth of sorrow we have felt. Add in the frenetic madness of materialism that has come to represent the holiday season, and we yearn to recall and revive genuine friendships and generosity, something deeper and more meaningful than tinsel and price tags. The holidays are hard on the grief stricken; there is just no way around it. We have suffered greatly this year and no presents or well wishes will abate our sorrow, yet contact with those we know and love is more important than ever. After all, those who served sacrificed for more than materialism and financial security; they sacrificed for freedom's sake and a way of life that included trusting communities where people truly cared for each other. And so this holiday season might be our time to retreat from the commercial madness, slow the pace down and spend some very special moments with people that mean something to us. The brisk air of winter calls for the warm hearts of loved ones.

And while many around us are making resolutions for the coming New Year, we are learning to keep promises at bay. We try to take each day as it comes. The beginning of a new year does not automatically call for a giant to-do list. It is rather a time to cultivate a simple, healthy sense of direction.

MEDITATION

This season, perhaps even as a gift to our loved ones, those with us and those deceased, we will live through holidays in a saner fashion, concentrated on people we care about and not on "things". Our main gift to those around us will be our presence instead of our presents.

We will also try to keep from getting caught up in elaborate plans or promises, living in each day and taking the best of each day. This season we will offer a bit more of ourselves to others. And when we are rewarded tenfold, we will not hide from the happiness.

Spring
A New Beginning

As winter wound down we looked to the coming season of new growth. Though we're frightened of the unknown, still the new blossoms, colorful and fresh, dot the landscape. With spring comes promise. The buds on the trees, the flowers in early bloom, the nearness of Creation, all are inspiring. Our inner beings long for a personal springtime to mimic the earth's new vitality. We learn from Creation that new life is a mainstay of Nature herself. So it is that we are inspired to renew ourselves in the spirit of hope, to look with fresh eyes at the world around us and see again the beauty we once knew. Just as those who served relied upon their brothers and sisters in service, so too many people have helped us get this far and we will continue to rely on their goodness. It is no weakness to call out for help; indeed sometimes it is a sign of strength and maturity. So, as we go about our new life, we make sure there is room for those who continue to be by our side, for there may be times they will need us, too. And we will be present for them as they have been for us.

Much was sacrificed so that new blossoms could flourish in the rich ground of springtime. Nor is our own suffering disconnected to the beauty of new growth, but is rather an indelible mark upon it, ever reminding us of how the love and caring of others has contributed to our well being.

MEDITATION

This spring as we appreciate the new growth around us, we will also appreciate the lives of those who have contributed to our being able to see beauty in the world and in ourselves. We will continue to remember those who served, especially our own loved one and this spring we will find ways to show our gratitude to those who have stayed close to us in difficult times. It's usually the little things that are so meaningful, and there are a lot of little things we can do quietly to show our sincere gratitude to the good people around us.

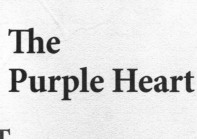

The Purple Heart

The Purple Heart award was created by General George Washington on August 7, 1782, during the Revolutionary War. It was originally called the Badge of Military Merit and consisted of a heart made of purple cloth and embroidered with the word "Merit." Only 3 Revolutionary War soldiers were awarded the badge, nevertheless, the award was never abolished and, about 150 years later, General Douglas MacArthur advocated a change in the name and design of the award. As a result, the Purple Heart medal was revived into its present form on the 200th Anniversary of George Washington's birth, February 22, 1932.

Today's Purple Heart medal consists of a deep purple heart shape framed by a gold border and overlaid with a profile of George Washington. Above the heart is his family coat of arms flanked by sprays of green leaves. The medal is suspended from a purple ribbon edged with thin white stripes.

The Purple Heart is awarded, in the name of the President of the United States, to members of the U.S. armed forces who are wounded by an instrument of war in the hands of the enemy and posthumously to the next of kin in the name of those who are killed in action or die of wounds received in action. The Purple Heart is deserved by virtue of having received the wound under the specified conditions, and does not necessarily require the recommendation of a commanding officer to be awarded.

George Washington's original order instituting the award included this phrase, "Let it be known that he who wears the Military Order of the Purple Heart has given of his blood in the defense of his homeland and shall forever be revered by his fellow countrymen."

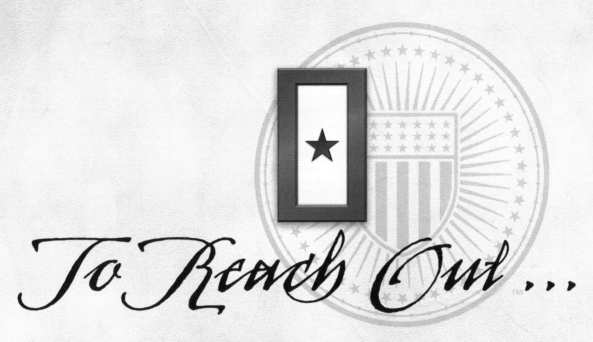

To Reach Out ...

Being of Assistance

As we pass through the natural stages of the grieving process an overwhelming sense of loneliness can and often does overtake us. The feeling of being isolated from even those we are normally close to is stark and very real. Though sometimes family members can be too close to provide the right kind of comfort or consolation, quite often only a family member has an actual feeling for the depth and complexity of our emotion surrounding the death in the family. Sometimes help may even come from a distant family member or one with whom we never formed a bond for some reason. So each family comes together as it can, attempting to communicate warm and heartfelt regards to each other. Whatever the form of familial relationships, somewhere in the mix of family is usually some hidden help in hard times.

There are times, even in the closest of families, however, when it may be more appropriate to seek guidance from an outside source. If you have grown up in an especially close family you know how sometimes an outsider, perhaps even a perfect stranger, can better address your deep distress and sorrow.

Fortunately, today, many funeral homes, as well as social and private agencies, conduct bereavement groups where one may share personal grief with others who are going through it. Remember too that the United States Office of Veterans Affairs offers bereavement counseling for the families of those who died in service of their country. Through the national office you can contact a Vet Center near you to obtain their free services. For the families of veterans who were no longer in service, the VA can refer you to other bereavement counseling resources in your area. Attending a bereavement group of this sort is in no way a denial of the important and meaningful role the family plays in comforting its own, nor is it a sign of an inability to foster the inner strength to face life's difficult times. Rather, attendance in a bereavement group can actually become a way in which grieving individuals can demonstrate their compassion for fellow sufferers, and thereby tap into their individual wells of inspiration and generosity of spirit.

★

Helpful Bereavement Resources

In the following pages we have provided a list of websites, books and organizations that may be of help to you in these difficult days. They represent a bare few of the resources available and some will be more appropriate than others. But all represent an effort to reach out to you in the sadness and sorrow you live with at the present time.

Many of those who served got into the habit of reading while in the service, perhaps in the long hours at sea or by lantern light at cot side. As human beings, we read because we are communicating creatures and our souls need the mental and spiritual nourishment that inspiring and insightful words can provide. In our grieving too, the act of reading can play an important role. We read what others have experienced. We read of the resiliency of the human spirit and about practical ways to cope with what has happened in our lives. And we read of a better time coming for us because someone has touched us with the written word. We have listed a handful of books that may provide a measure of identification, consolation and hope.

There are also organizations founded, often by those responding to their own bereavement issues, for the express purpose of helping and guiding individuals in their grief. These organizations may specialize in one or another grief related issues or they may be a general store not only of information and empathy, but also of practical ways to cope with the loss of a loved one. A list is provided here.

Today few schoolchildren could finish their homework without the computer and the ease of research afforded by the internet. Handy information on just about any topic is right at our fingertips. Perhaps it would be wise for us to see what help is available in this venue to our families. To that purpose, we have provided just a few websites specific to grief and the grief process. Many of these sites represent a community of people who have gathered to share some of the most compelling lessons of a lifetime.

★

Helpful Reading

A Grief Observed by C.S. Lewis

In this classic of grief literature, the great Oxford don and famed Christian apologist reflects in an intensely personal manner upon the death of his wife and the subsequent grief that forced him to look deeper into the workings of his own heart and soul.

Military Widow: A Survivor's Guide by Joanne M. Steen and M. Regina Asaro

A nationally certified counselor and the widow of a naval aviator killed in the line of duty along with a psychiatric nurse and crisis responder have created a comprehensive survival guide for widows of service personnel that can also benefit other family members. The volume combines profiles of military widows and their response to loss with accompanying insight into the unique world of the military.

The Mourning Handbook: The Most Comprehensive Resource Offering Practical and Compassionate Advice on Coping with All Aspects of Death and Dying by Helen Fitzgerald

The author covers the complexities of grief in relation to the special needs of those who have lost a loved one in unique circumstances. It offers practical assistance and emotional companionship and is designed to be highly accessible to those mourning a loss. Having counseled with thousands who have experienced personal loss, Helen Fitzgerald adeptly reaches out especially to those who are facing the aftermath of traumatic situations.

On Grief and Grieving: Finding the Meaning of Grief Through the Five Stages of Loss by Elisabeth Kubler-Ross and David Kessler

The famed author of *On Death and Dying* combined with author David Kessler before her own death to further examine how the stages of death: denial, anger, bargaining, depression and acceptance apply to our own grieving process.

★

Sad Isn't Bad: A Good Grief Guidebook for Kids dealing With Loss
by Michaelene Munday, illustrated by R.W. Alley

Because children cope with loss in their own unique ways, this volume, written with sensitivity by school counselor Michaelene Munday and illustrated warmly by R.W.Alley, addresses in a positive way the particular emotional needs of children as they grieve, including reassurances that the world is a safe place, that life is good and that the pain of loss does subside as our hearts mend.

The Healing Journey Through Grief: Your Journal for Reflection and Recovery
By Phil Rich

Professional counselor Phil Rich uses the healing power of writing in this very special journal to help those who have lost a loved one sort through the many and varied manifestations of grief. While supplying pertinent information about the grieving process, the volume also uses the journal format to allow mourners the opportunity to bring together disparate emotions, thoughts, memories and reflections in one place and experience the powerful healing potential in such an ongoing exercise.

The Wall by Eve Bunting, illustrated by Ronald Himmler

For ages 4-8, this beautifully written and illustrated picture book is the story of a boy who visits the Vietnam War Memorial with his father in order to find his grandfather's name. The poignant story of family, patriotism and loss is a stirring portrayal that can be used with children to explore the reality of death and sacrifice.

Man's Search for Meaning by Victor Frankl

According to famed psychiatrist ,Victor Frankl, our deepest desire as human beings is to find purpose and meaning in our lives. This philosophy was hard won in the author's imprisonment in the concentration camps of World War II Germany, including Auschwitz, and became the basis for his system of psychotherapy. This well known volume is a fascinating, moving and powerful testament to the innate resiliency of the human spirit.

★

I Wasn't Ready to Say Goodbye: Surviving, Coping and Healing After the Sudden Death of a Loved One by Brook Noel and Pamela D. Blair, Ph.D

This is the updated version of a well known work on bereavement by two women who have suffered the sudden loss of a loved one. The volume covers a variety of topics and reflects the challenges of unexpected death and the many ways it affects our grief. It also contains new material on various grieving styles, the roles of religion and faith in the grieving process, among other helpful topics. This is a valuable and comforting resource for most difficult times.

Surviving Grief ... and Learning to Live Again by Catherine M. Sanders

Dr. Sanders writes from personal experience and scholarly research but also with an uncommon compassion about the realities of the grieving process. She takes us through what she describes as the five universal phases of grief and shares valuable insights into the factors that influence our grief. This is a thorough, empathetic and profound look at our own humanity as seen in the ways we attend to our sorrow and loss.

Chicken Soup for the Grieving Soul: Stories About Life, Death and Overcoming the Loss of a Loved One by Jack Canfield and Mark Victor Hansen

Part of the now famous Chicken Soup collection, this collection of inspirational stories from those who have experienced loss emphasizes the communal aspect of grief in that it speaks to the essential sharing and togetherness fostered in bereavement. Specific topics about coping with death and the tender, soothing, encouraging stories touch the heart in a most helpful and comforting way.

★

Helpful Organizations

No Greater Love

Founded because of a promise made to a dying soldier, No Greater Love is a humanitarian organization dedicated to providing annual programs of remembrance, friendship and care for families who lost a loved one in the service of our country or by an act of terrorism. Tel. (202) 783-4665.

The Grief Recovery Institute

An internationally recognized authority on grief recovery, with training programs, a Grief Recovery Handbook, as well as outreach, certification and community education programs. Tel. (818) 907-9600.

The American Hospice Foundation

The American Hospice Foundation aids programs that serve the needs of the terminally ill and grieving individuals of all ages. Initiatives include: guidance for caregivers of the terminally ill, educational campaigns to aid bereaved employees and co-workers, training and materials on grieving for teachers and school counselors, educational programs for clergy and workshops for hospice staff and others serving grieving families. Tel. (800) 347-1413.

Renew: Center for Personal Recovery

Specialists in crisis management for schools and other organizations. Renew offers services for individuals, families and organizations experiencing any kind of trauma or loss. Educational resources and workshops available. Tel. (513) 376-9954.

The National Funeral Directors Association

The NFDA has many grief resources available as well as grief related materials and has an online resource store with downloadable information, videos and CD's as well as an array of brochure material related to grief issues. Tel. (800) 228-6332.

Survivors of Suicide

SOS is a bereavement support and information division of the American Association of Suicidology, an organization that is dedicated to the understanding and prevention of suicide. Tel. (202) 237-2280.

Helpful Websites

www.GriefNet.org

GriefNet.org is an Internet community of persons dealing with grief, death, and major loss. Directed by Dr. Cendra Lynn, Ph.D., who is a clinical psychologist and certified Traumatologist, GriefNet is a well-known part of a non-profit organization with an array of resources for the bereaved that also operates an independent companion site, KIDSAID.com, for children and their parents.

www.centering.org

The Centering Corporation is a non-profit 501(C) 3 organization dedicated to providing education on grief and loss for professionals and the families they serve. Founded in 1977 by Joy and Dr. Marvin Johnson, it continues to provide educational offerings, bookstores, and workshops for caregivers and families.

www.WidowNet

WidowNet is the original online information and self-help resource for, and by, widows and widowers. Topics covered include grief, bereavement, recovery, and other helpful information. WidowNet facilitates communication between people about their shared experiences of grief, survival, and recovery.

www.bereavementmag.com

The online version of Bereavement Magazine: A Journal of Hope and Healing. Designed to be "a support group in print," Bereavement Magazine includes articles, stories and poetry. Readers have full access to archived issues at this website, as well as access to some material available only on the web.

www.thecompassionatefriends.org

The mission of The Compassionate Friends is to assist families toward the positive resolution of grief following the death of a child of any age and to provide information to help others be supportive. Each chapter, along with the supporting National Office, is committed to helping every

★

bereaved parent, sibling, or grandparent who reaches out to them. Today more than 600 chapters serving all 50 states plus Washington D.C. and Puerto Rico offer friendship, understanding, and hope to bereaved parents, siblings, grandparents, and other family members during the natural grieving process.

www.journeyofhearts.org

A unique web experience that combines elements of medicine, psychiatry, poetry, prose and images to provide resources and support to those who have experienced loss, be it acute or long-standing. Designed for those who are in the early stages of grief, loss and bereavement to provide words of solace, condolence, hope and inspiration, the site utilizes a concept they call *Transitional Medicine* to help visitors through the grief process. It is also for those who are ready to start healing after a significant loss, accept, assimilate, and recover from the loss.

www.sesameworkshop.org/grief

Sesame Workshop is a nonprofit educational organization making a meaningful difference in the lives of children worldwide by addressing their critical developmental needs. The Workshop develops innovative and engaging educational content delivered in a variety of ways — including television, radio, books, magazines, interactive media, and community outreach. *When Families Grieve* is part of the workshop designed to help grieving families and contains a component especially for military families. To find out how to request *When Families Grieve* kits, use grief@sesameworkshop.org. *When Families Grieve* kits for military families are also available through *Militaryonesource.com*.

www.remember.gov

The White House Commission on Remembrance, established by Congress in 2000, is an independent, non-partisan government agency that encourages Americans to honor the sacrifices of our fallen and their families. It promotes acts of remembrance throughout the year and asks citizens to pay our debt of gratitude in memory of those who died in service to our country by giving something back to the nation.

★

Finding Help

Remember that your local funeral directors can always provide essential information and can be a very helpful resource. They have most likely performed military funerals on a regular basis and are familiar with memorial customs associated with the military.

In addition to the general aids in bereavement, the following is a special military help and information section intended to assist the family in obtaining information, documents and items concerning the deceased veteran. It should be noted that this section is not intended to be a definitive resource but rather an aid that will help guide the family in the right direction to obtain information or to suggest agencies and locations that may be of assistance. Lined pages at the end of this section are provided to keep notes, names, phone numbers and websites for ready recall as you begin your research. This may prove especially useful in relation to websites which can often be redesigned, relocated or updated in their procedures or policies.

Research Information & Special Items Available

DD 214 – This one page document is a brief summary of the veteran's service and contains most of the information necessary to process other requests. *(Note: This is probably the single most important document you can obtain because it will not only give you information about the deceased veteran but also expedite obtaining other records and items.)*

Medical and Health Records – Medical treatment received while in the military service.

Replacement Medals, Awards and Decorations

Headstone/grave marker – An inscribed headstone / grave marker or a medallion to affix to privately purchased headstone / marker.

Presidential Memorial Certificate – A certificate to honor the memory of an honorably discharged deceased veteran signed by the President.

Other resources – Additional information for possible assistance and direction in your search.

★

Applying for Information

It should be noted that for the purpose of obtaining military records, medical records, and other items of a deceased veteran, researchers are divided into two categories, *General Public* and *Next of Kin*.

GENERAL PUBLIC

Information released to the general public is very limited but a good place to begin is:

http://www.archives.gov/st-louis/military-personnel/public/general-public.html

This website will give an overview of the information that is available to the general public and has detailed instructions on how to submit requests, what basic information is required to process a request and what costs may be involved. There is also a link to "Standard Form (SF) 180, Request pertaining to Military Records" which must be used by the general public.

NEXT OF KIN

For next of kin, you may also use a simplified online request form called **eVetRecs** which is available only to veterans and the next of kin of a deceased veteran. It can be used to obtain free copies of a deceased relative's service records including military service record, medical records and other information concerning the deceased veteran.

For the purpose of obtaining copies of a deceased veteran's military records, the next of kin is defined as follows:

Surviving spouse *(that has not remarried)*	Mother	Brother
	Son	Sister
Father	Daughter	

★

Services & Resources

For Veterans' Families, Dependents and Next of Kin

National Archives

http://www.archives.gov/

An excellent source for the next of kin can be found in the National Archives at the website listed above. Under the section entitled *Veterans' Service Records* you will find a number of items that are available to the next of kin which can be accessed by the aforementioned simplified online request form **eVet Recs**. Also, this one location is an excellent place to start and can provide information on:

• Military Service Records (DD Form 214)
• Replacement Medals, Decorations or Awards
• Veterans Medical and Health Records
• Frequently Asked Questions

eVetRecs

Once you click on "Request records online with **eVetRecs**" and prior to actually launching the request for any information through **eVetRecs**, review the brief description of the online request form to give you a basic understanding of how the process works. You should gather as much information as you can about the deceased veteran. Take the time to review all the information that details how to use **eVetRecs** by scrolling down the page before clicking on the **eVetRecs** launch button. You will find a great deal of information, including an *eVetRecs help and FAQ* link to further assist you. *(Note: Forms and information can change over time and always use the current instructions found on the websites for any of the forms or requests you make).*

You will be asked to identify your relationship to the deceased, the branch of service, component (active, reserve), officer or enlisted, and your

★

category of request or what you are seeking such as personal military (report of separation – DD-214), medical, etc.)

The more information you have obtained in advance, (full name used in military, social security number, place of birth, approximate date the veteran left service, service number if applicable, etc.) the easier it will be to successfully process your request.

You will also be asked whether you are requesting an <u>undeleted</u> or <u>deleted</u> personal military history. Definitions are provided after each term. While the choice is yours, note that the undeleted version is ordinarily required to determine eligibility for benefits.

Lastly, you must print the form and then sign and date the signature verification area of the customized form. (If you do not have a printer, follow the instructions to hand write the verification). This is very important because the Privacy Act of 1974 (5 U.S.C. 552a) requires that all requests for records and information must be submitted in writing. As the next of kin of a deceased veteran, you must provide proof of death of the veteran such as a copy of the death certificate, letter from funeral home or published obituary. Each request must be signed and dated (with proof of death) and the signature verification form must be mailed or faxed within twenty (20) days of submitting your **eVetRecs** request or your request will be removed from the system.

Note: if you are unable to complete the **eVetRecs** process due to limited information you have on the deceased veteran, or are requesting something that is not available through **eVetRecs** you always have the option to use the "Standard Form (SF) 180, Request pertaining to Military Records" and identify yourself as next of kin (with proof of death).

DD 214
Certificate of Release or Discharge from Active Duty

As stated earlier, this personal military history is probably the first item you may wish to obtain. Sometimes referred to as Proof of Service, this single document is a synopsis of service and contains many vital pieces of information about the veteran including:

- Date and place of entry into active duty
- Home address at time of entry
- Date and place of release from active duty
- Home address after separation
- Last duty assignment and rank
- Military job specialty
- Military education
- Decorations, medals, badges, citations and campaign awards
- Total creditable service
- Foreign service credited
- Separation information (type of separation, character of service, authority and reason for separation, separation and reenlistment eligibility codes)

(Note: prior to January 1, 1950, several similar forms with different designations were used by the military services.)

Since most other requests and organizations generally require some proof of service, the DD 214 is the most obvious place to start gathering information. Once you have the copy of the DD 214 with service number and all other information, it can expedite other requests.

Military Medical and Health Records
http://www.archives.gov/

Information on Military Medical and Health Records can be found at a link under *Veterans' Service Records*. Medical records cover outpatient, dental and mental health treatment which a former member received while in the military service. These health record documents include induction and separation, physical examinations and routine medical care (doctor/dental visits, lab tests, etc.) when the patient was not admitted to a hospital. Next of kin may use the simplified **eVetRecs** or the Standard Form 180. There is generally no charge for the records but if any fee is required, you will be notified.

★

Clinical (hospital inpatient) records are filed separately as are many health records. For further information see the detailed explanation at *Medical and Health Records.*

Replacement Medals and Awards
http://www.archives.gov/

Information on requesting replacement military service medals, decorations and awards can be found under *Veterans' Service Records* in the section *Replace Lost Medals and Awards.* Requests are directed to the specific branch of the military in which the veteran served using "Standard Form (SF) 180, Request pertaining to Military Records" however, several branches can also be submitted via **eVetRecs**. For specifics on services, see information contained in the section *Replace Lost Medals and Awards.* Remember that, as next of kin, you will have to attach Proof of Death as was discussed earlier.

However, it would still be prudent to first have a DD-214 as documented proof of the deceased veteran being awarded the medal and attach a copy of this to your SF-180 request. Also, should criteria for replacement medals change or even be eliminated, you still will have a record of the award and can pursue other avenues to replace the medal.

Headstones, Markers or Medallions

Eligible veterans are entitled to an inscribed headstone or marker, inscribed with certain information about the deceased veteran for any *unmarked grave.* For eligible veterans whose death occurred on or after November 1, 1990, the VA may provide a headstone / marker or medallion even if the grave is already marked with a private one. For current information on what defines an eligible veteran, who may submit the request and further details including frequently asked questions, what information is on the headstone or marker, etc. go to:

http://www.cem.va.gov/

★

Under Burial and Memorial Benefits you will see the link to *Headstones, Markers and Medallions*. It should be noted that the list of those eligible to apply for a government headstone, marker or medallion from the National Cemetery Administration is greatly expanded compared to the limited list of next of kin that may apply for a deceased veteran's records. A complete list of those eligible can be found under the application process.

The headstones come in granite or marble. Flat markers are available in bronze, granite or marble. This headstone or marker will be delivered at no cost, anywhere in the world. (Note: before ordering, check with the cemetery to ensure that the Government-furnished headstone or marker will be accepted. All installation fees are the responsibility of the applicant).

Another alternative for families of veterans with a privately purchased headstone or marker (and the veteran's death occurred on or after November 1, 1990) is to request a medallion that can be affixed to the headstone/marker. This bronze marker comes in three sizes, 5, 3, or 1 ½ inches. Each medallion has the word "VETERAN" across the top and the branch of service across the bottom. Each medallion comes with appropriate adhesives, hardware and instructions. All installation fees are the responsibility of the applicant.

This website also contains a link to the application form and instructions on how to complete the necessary forms, what information is necessary and what documents need to be attached.

Presidential Memorial Certificate

A Presidential Memorial Certificate is an engraved paper certificate signed by the current President of the United States, to honor the memory of honorably discharged deceased veterans. The certificate may be requested by next of kin and loved ones. More than one certificate may be provided. This program is administered by the Department of Veterans Affairs (VA). For further information on how to apply, required documentation and an application form, visit the Department of Veterans Affairs website for Presidential Memorial Certificates at:

http://www.cem.va.gov/pmc.asp

or, you may also access the site through:

http://www.cem.va.gov/

Click on the Presidential Memorial Certificate and it will provide detailed instructions on how to apply for this certificate including the accompanying documents required. These include a copy of the deceased veteran's honorable discharge certificate or the DD-214 showing "honorable" and a copy of the death certificate attached for the request to be processed. Make sure you submit copies only as documents will not be returned to you. You may mail your request to the address on the Presidential Memorial Certificate form or use the fax number at the bottom of the form. There is no charge for this certificate.

Other Helpful Sites

http://www.archives.gov/

The National Archives site (listed directly above) has links to numerous other helpful sites that will be of interest to the family of a deceased veteran. The *Veterans' FAQ* section not only gives useful information on a variety of subjects but also provides telephone numbers for help or immediate assistance from several agencies. In addition, there are a number of resources available containing histories, photos, information and other military research links.

NOTES The following pages are designed specifically to provide you with a ready and permanent place to keep valuable telephone numbers, names, websites, and addresses for future reference and follow up.

_____

_____

_____

_____

_____

_____

_____

_____

_____

_____

Thank You

May we take this space to thank you, for we know that in the days and weeks that have passed you have demonstrated to those around you the redeeming qualities of bearing one's grief with honesty and grace. You have helped someone without knowing it, someone who was watching as you trudged through your sorrow, deeply hurt, but marching forward to bring a measure of the love you have known in your life to others in need of it. You have also been *one who served*.

You have thanked others for their care and concern for you in your difficult time. You have shown the worth of gratitude by employing it in your own life. We thank you for this expression as we also thank those who made this keepsake volume available. This volume bears the hopes of many, that they could bring to you a measure of comfort and consolation. In the spirit of service to country, in the spirit of gratitude for the gifts of freedom and for the lives lived and lost in that cause, all involved in the creation and distribution of *One Who Served* thank you for enduring your burdens as you have, and thereby demonstrating to others that it can be done and that there is something beyond the day's woe and the night's tears. Thank you for helping show us all the way of hope. Thank you for the family you have made, the sacrifices you have borne and the tribute you have paid to your loved one, the very special…one who served.

One Who Served Creative Team

TEXT
John Sydney Tighe
Mr. Tighe is the creator of numerous special edition books relating to inspirational and value oriented themes. These include publications with a wide range of audiences from youth to business leaders.

TEXT
Robert P. Giers
From 1966 to 1970, Mr. Giers served in the United States Marine Corps Reserve as a Naval Aviator achieving the rank of Captain. He is a Vietnam veteran having served a tour of duty in 1968-1969.

TEXT
BMCM (SW) Edward F. Gallagher, IV, USNR, ret.
Master Chief Gallagher began his 28 year naval career in 1972, first on active duty and then in the United States Naval Reserve. He retired in 2006 at the rank of Master Chief Petty Officer and is a Vietnam and Iraqi Freedom veteran.

ART/DESIGN/LAYOUT
Christopher Pelicano
Mr. Pelicano (A.R.T. Services) has more than 30 years of freelance experience in graphic design, illustration, and creative problem solving, including 16 years as a staff artist providing concept design and art direction for many Fortune 500 companies.

PRODUCTION
John Addy
Mr. Addy has a long history involving the coordination, production and manufacturing of printed matter. His expertise spans a multitude of projects including special publications and book publishing.